POLLYANNA

By ELEANOR H. PORTER

AUTHOR OF

"Cross Currents," "The Turn of the Tides," etc.

A. L. BURT COMPANY

Publishers   New York

Published by arrangement with The Page Company

Printed in U. S. A.

"POLLYANNA SAT SO STILL SHE HARDLY SEEMED TO BREATHE."

TO
My Cousin Belle

CONTENTS

Contents

POLLYANNA

——•——

CHAPTER I

MISS POLLY

MISS POLLY HARRINGTON entered her kitchen a
little hurriedly this June morning. Miss Polly did
not usually make hurried movements; she specially
prided herself on her repose of manner. But to-day
she was hurrying — actually hurrying.

Nancy, washing dishes at the sink, looked up in
surprise. Nancy had been working in Miss Polly's
kitchen only two months, but already she knew that
her mistress did not usually hurry.

" Nancy! "

" Yes, ma'am." Nancy answered cheerfully, but
she still continued wiping the pitcher in her hand.

" Nancy," — Miss Polly's voice was very stern
now — " when I'm talking to you, I wish you to

stop your work and listen to what I have to say."

Nancy flushed miserably. She set the pitcher down at once, with the cloth still about it, thereby nearly tipping it over — which did not add to her composure.

" Yes, ma'am; I will, ma'am," she stammered, righting the pitcher, and turning hastily. " I was only keepin' on with my work 'cause you specially told me this mornin' ter hurry with my dishes, ye know."

Her mistress frowned.

" That will do, Nancy. I did not ask for explanations. I asked for your attention."

" Yes, ma'am." Nancy stifled a sigh. She was wondering if ever in any way she could please this woman. Nancy had never " worked out " before; but a sick mother suddenly widowed and left with three younger children besides Nancy herself, had forced the girl into doing something toward their support, and she had been so pleased when she found a place in the kitchen of the great house on the hill — Nancy had come from " The Corners," six miles away, and she knew Miss Polly Harring-ton only as the mistress of the old Harrington home-stead, and one of the wealthiest residents of the town. That was two months before. She knew Miss Polly now as a stern, severe-faced woman who frowned if a knife clattered to the floor, or if a door banged — but who never thought to smile even when knives and doors were still.

"When you've finished your morning work, Nancy," Miss Polly was saying now, "you may clear the little room at the head of the stairs in the attic, and make up the cot bed. Sweep the room and clean it, of course, after you clear out the trunks and boxes."

"Yes, ma'am. And where shall I put the things, please, that I take out?"

"In the front attic." Miss Polly hesitated, then went on: "I suppose I may as well tell you now, Nancy. My niece, Miss Pollyanna Whittier, is coming to live with me. She is eleven years old, and will sleep in that room."

"A little girl — coming here, Miss Harrington? Oh, won't that be nice!" cried Nancy, thinking of the sunshine her own little sisters made in the home at "The Corners."

"Nice? Well, that isn't exactly the word I should use," rejoined Miss Polly, stiffly. "However, I intend to make the best of it, of course. I am a good woman, I hope; and I know my duty."

Nancy colored hotly.

"Of course, ma'am; it was only that I thought a little girl here might — might brighten things up — for you," she faltered.

"Thank you," rejoined the lady, dryly. "I can't say, however, that I see any immediate need for that."

"But, of course, you — you'd want her, your sister's child," ventured Nancy, vaguely feeling that somehow she must prepare a welcome for this lonely little stranger.

Miss Polly lifted her chin haughtily.

"Well, really, Nancy, just because I happened to have a sister who was silly enough to marry and bring unnecessary children into a world that was already quite full enough, I can't see how I should particularly *want* to have the care of them myself. However, as I said before, I hope I know my duty. See that you clean the corners, Nancy," she finished sharply, as she left the room.

"Yes, ma'am," sighed Nancy, picking up the half-dried pitcher — now so cold it must be rinsed again.

In her own room, Miss Polly took out once more the letter which she had received two days before from the far-away Western town, and which had been so unpleasant a surprise to her. The letter was addressed to Miss Polly Harrington, Beldingsville, Vermont; and it read as follows:

"DEAR MADAM:— I regret to inform you that the Rev. John Whittier died two weeks ago, leaving one child, a girl eleven years old. He left practically nothing else save a few books; for, as you doubtless know, he was the pastor of this small mission church, and had a very meagre salary.

"I believe he was your deceased sister's husband, but he gave me to understand the families were not on the best of terms. He thought, however, that for your sister's sake you might wish to take the child and bring her up among her own people in the East. Hence I am writing to you.

"The little girl will be all ready to start by the time you get this letter; and if you can take her, we would appreciate it very much if you would write that she might come at once, as there is a man and his wife here who are going East very soon, and they would take her with them to Boston, and put her on the Beldingsville train. Of course you would be notified what day and train to expect Pollyanna on.

" Hoping to hear favorably from you soon, I
remain,

" Respectfully yours,

" JEREMIAH O. WHITE."

With a frown Miss Polly folded the letter and
tucked it into its envelope. She had answered it the
day before, and she had said she would take the
child, of course. She *hoped* she knew her duty well
enough for that! — disagreeable as the task would
be.

As she sat now, with the letter in her hands, her
thoughts went back to her sister, Jennie, who had
been this child's mother, and to the time when Jennie, as a girl of twenty, had insisted upon marrying
the young minister, in spite of her family's remon-
strances. There had been a man of wealth who had
wanted her — and the family had much preferred
him to the minister; but Jennie had not. The man
of wealth had more years, as well as more money,
to his credit, while the minister had only a young
head full of youth's ideals and enthusiasm, and a
heart full of love. Jennie had preferred these —
quite naturally, perhaps; so she had married the
minister, and had gone south with him as a home
missionary's wife.

The break had come then. Miss Polly remembered it well, though she had been but a girl of fifteen, the youngest, at the time. The family had had little more to do with the missionary's wife. To be sure, Jennie herself had written, for a time, and had named her last baby " Pollyanna " for her two sisters, Polly and Anna — the other babies had all died. This had been the last time that Jennie had written; and in a few years there had come the news of her death, told in a short, but heart-broken little note from the minister himself, dated at a little town in the West.

Meanwhile, time had not stood still for the occupants of the great house on the hill. Miss Polly, looking out at the far-reaching valley below, thought of the changes those twenty-five years had brought to her.

She was forty now, and quite alone in the world. Father, mother, sisters — all were dead. For years, now, she had been sole mistress of the house and of the thousands left her by her father. There were people who had openly pitied her lonely life, and who had urged her to have some friend or companion to live with her; but she had not welcomed either their sympathy or their advice. She was not lonely, she said. She liked being by herself. She preferred quiet. But now —

Miss Polly rose with frowning face and closely-shut lips. She was glad, of course, that she was a good woman, and that she not only knew her duty, but had sufficient strength of character to perform it. But — *Pollyanna!* — what a ridiculous name!

CHAPTER II

OLD TOM AND NANCY

In the little attic room Nancy swept and scrubbed vigorously, paying particular attention to the corners. There were times, indeed, when the vigor she put into her work was more of a relief to her feelings than it was an ardor to efface dirt — Nancy, in spite of her frightened submission to her mistress, was no saint.

"I — just — wish — I could — dig — out — the corners — of — her — soul!" she muttered jerkily, punctuating her words with murderous jabs of her pointed cleaning-stick. "There's plenty of 'em needs cleanin' all right, all right! The idea of stickin' that blessed child 'way off up here in this hot little room — with no fire in the winter, too; and all this big house ter pick and choose from! Unnecessary children, indeed! Humph!" snapped Nancy, wringing her rag so hard her fingers ached from the strain; "I guess it ain't *children* what is *most* unnecessary just now, just now!"

9

For some time she worked in silence; then, her task finished, she looked about the bare little room in plain disgust.

"Well, it's done — my part, anyhow," she sighed. "There ain't no dirt here — and there's mighty little else. Poor little soul! — a pretty place this is ter put a homesick, lonesome child into!" she finished, going out and closing the door with a bang. "Oh!" she ejaculated, biting her lip. Then, doggedly: "Well, I don't care. I hope she did hear the bang — I do, I do!"

In the garden that afternoon, Nancy found a few minutes in which to interview Old Tom, who had pulled the weeds and shovelled the paths about the place for uncounted years.

"Mr. Tom," began Nancy, throwing a quick glance over her shoulder to make sure she was unobserved; "did you know a little girl was comin' here ter live with Miss Polly?"

"A — what?" demanded the old man, straightening his bent back with difficulty.

"A little girl — to live with Miss Polly."

"Go on with yer jokin'," scoffed unbelieving Tom. "Why don't ye tell me the sun is a-goin' ter set in the east ter-morrer?"

"But it's true. She told me so herself," maintained Nancy. "It's her niece; and she's eleven years old."

The man's jaw fell.

"Sho! — I wonder, now," he muttered; then a tender light came into his faded eyes. "It ain't — but it must be — Miss Jennie's little gal! There wasn't none of the rest of 'em married. Why, Nancy, it must be Miss Jennie's little gal. Glory be ter praise! ter think of my old eyes a-seein' this!"

"Who was Miss Jennie?"

"She was an angel straight out of Heaven," breathed the man, fervently; "but the old master and missus knew her as their oldest daughter. She was twenty when she married and went away from here long years ago. Her babies all died, I heard, except the last one; and that must be the one what's a-comin'."

"She's eleven years old."

"Yes, she might be," nodded the old man.

"And she's goin' ter sleep in the attic — more shame ter *her!*" scolded Nancy, with another glance over her shoulder toward the house behind her.

Old Tom frowned. The next moment a curious smile curved his lips.

" I'm a-wonderin' what Miss Polly will do with a child in the house," he said.

" Humph! Well, *I*'m a-wonderin' what a child will do with Miss Polly in the house!" snapped Nancy.

The old man laughed.

" I'm afraid you ain't fond of Miss Polly," he grinned.

" As if ever anybody could be fond of her!" scorned Nancy.

Old Tom smiled oddly. He stooped and began to work again.

" I guess maybe you didn't know about Miss Polly's love affair," he said slowly.

" Love affair — *her!* No! — and I guess nobody else didn't, neither."

" Oh, yes they did," nodded the old man. " And the feller's livin' ter-day — right in this town, too."

" Who is he? "

" I ain't a-tellin' that. It ain't fit that I should." The old man drew himself erect. In his dim blue eyes, as he faced the house, there was the loyal servant's honest pride in the family he has served and loved for long years.

" But it don't seem possible — her and a lover," still maintained Nancy.

Old Tom shook his head.

"You didn't know Miss Polly as I did," he argued. "She used ter be real handsome — and she would be now, if she'd let herself be."

"Handsome! Miss Polly!"

"Yes. If she'd just let that tight hair of hern all out loose and careless-like, as it used ter be, and wear the sort of bunnits with posies in 'em, and the kind o' dresses all lace and white things — you'd see she'd be handsome! Miss Polly ain't old, Nancy."

"Ain't she, though? Well, then she's got an awfully good imitation of it — she has, she has!" sniffed Nancy.

"Yes, I know. It begun then — at the time of the trouble with her lover," nodded Old Tom; "and it seems as if she'd been feedin' on wormwood an' thistles ever since — she's that bitter an' prickly ter deal with."

"I should say she was," declared Nancy, indignantly. "There's no pleasin' her, nohow, no matter how you try! I wouldn't stay if 'twa'n't for the wages and the folks at home what's needin' 'em. But some day — some day I shall jest b'ile over; and when I do, of course it'll be good-by Nancy for me. It will, it will."

Old Tom shook his head.

" I know. I've felt it. It's nart'ral — but 'tain't best, child; 'tain't best. Take my word for it, 'tain't best." And again he bent his old head to the work before him.

" Nancy!" called a sharp voice.

" Y-yes, ma'am," stammered Nancy; and hurried toward the house.

CHAPTER III

THE COMING OF POLLYANNA

In due time came the telegram announcing that Pollyanna would arrive in Beldingsville the next day, the twenty-fifth of June, at four o'clock. Miss Polly read the telegram, frowned, then climbed the stairs to the attic room. She still frowned as she looked about her.

The room contained a small bed, neatly made, two straight-backed chairs, a washstand, a bureau — without any mirror — and a small table. There were no drapery curtains at the dormer windows, no pictures on the wall. All day the sun had been pouring down upon the roof, and the little room was like an oven for heat. As there were no screens, the windows had not been raised. A big fly was buzzing angrily at one of them now, up and down, up and down, trying to get out.

Miss Polly killed the fly, swept it through the window (raising the sash an inch for the purpose),

15

straightened a chair, frowned again, and left the room.

"Nancy," she said a few minutes later, at the kitchen door, "I found a fly up-stairs in Miss Pollyanna's room. The window must have been raised at some time. I have ordered screens, but until they come I shall expect you to see that the windows remain closed. My niece will arrive to-morrow at four o'clock. I desire you to meet her at the station. Timothy will take the open buggy and drive you over. The telegram says 'light hair, red-checked gingham dress, and straw hat.' That is all I know, but I think it is sufficient for your purpose."

"Yes, ma'am; but — you — "

Miss Polly evidently read the pause aright, for she frowned and said crisply:

"No, I shall not go. It is not necessary that I should, I think. That is all." And she turned away — Miss Polly's arrangements for the comfort of her niece, Pollyanna, were complete.

In the kitchen, Nancy sent her flatiron with a vicious dig across the dish-towel she was ironing.

"'Light hair, red-checked gingham dress, and straw hat' — all she knows, indeed! Well, I'd be ashamed ter own it up, that I would, I would —

and her my onliest niece what was a-comin' from
'way across the continent!"

Promptly at twenty minutes to four the next
afternoon Timothy and Nancy drove off in the open
buggy to meet the expected guest. Timothy was
Old Tom's son. It was sometimes said in the town
that if Old Tom was Miss Polly's right-hand man,
Timothy was her left.

Timothy was a good-natured youth, and a good-
looking one, as well. Short as had been Nancy's
stay at the house, the two were already good
friends. To-day, however, Nancy was too full of
her mission to be her usual talkative self; and almost in silence she took the drive to the station and
alighted to wait for the train.

Over and over in her mind she was saying it —
"light hair, red-checked dress, straw hat." Over
and over again she was wondering just what sort
of child this Pollyanna was, anyway.

"I hope for her sake she's quiet and sensible, and
don't drop knives nor bang doors," she sighed to
Timothy, who had sauntered up to her.

"Well, if she ain't, nobody knows what'll become of the rest of us," grinned Timothy. "Imagine Miss Polly and a *noisy* kid! Gorry! there
goes the whistle now!"

" Oh, Timothy, I — I think it was mean ter send me," chattered the suddenly frightened Nancy, as she turned and hurried to a point where she could best watch the passengers alight at the little station.

It was not long before Nancy saw her — the slender little girl in the red-checked gingham with two fat braids of flaxen hair hanging down her back. Beneath the straw hat, an eager, freckled little face turned to the right and to the left, plainly searching for some one.

Nancy knew the child at once, but not for some time could she control her shaking knees sufficiently to go to her. The little girl was standing quite by herself when Nancy finally did approach her.

" Are you Miss — Pollyanna? " she faltered. The next moment she found herself half smothered in the clasp of two gingham-clad arms.

" Oh, I'm so glad, *glad,* GLAD to see you," cried an eager voice in her ear. " Of course I'm Polly-anna, and I'm so glad you came to meet me! I hoped you would."

" You — you did? " stammered Nancy, vaguely wondering how Pollyanna could possibly have known her — and wanted her. " You — you did? " she repeated, trying to straighten her hat.

" Oh, yes; and I've been wondering all the **way**

here what you looked like," cried the little girl, dancing on her toes, and sweeping the embarrassed Nancy from head to foot, with her eyes. " And now I know, and I'm glad you look just like you do look."

Nancy was relieved just then to have Timothy come up. Pollyanna's words had been most confusing.

" This is Timothy. Maybe you have a trunk," she stammered.

" Yes, I have," nodded Pollyanna, importantly. " I've got a brand-new one. The Ladies' Aid bought it for me — and wasn't it lovely of them, when they wanted the carpet so? Of course I don't know how much red carpet a trunk could buy, but it ought to buy some, anyhow — much as half an aisle, don't you think? I've got a little thing here in my bag that Mr. Gray said was a check, and that I must give it to you before I could get my trunk. Mr. Gray is Mrs. Gray's husband. They're cousins of Deacon Carr's wife. I came East with them, and they're lovely! And — there, here 'tis," she finished, producing the check after much fumbling in the bag she carried.

Nancy drew a long breath. Instinctively she felt that some one had to draw one — after that speech.

Then she stole a glance at Timothy. Timothy's eyes were studiously turned away.

The three were off at last, with Pollyanna's trunk in behind, and Pollyanna herself snugly ensconced between Nancy and Timothy. During the whole process of getting started, the little girl had kept up an uninterrupted stream of comments and questions, until the somewhat dazed Nancy found herself quite out of breath trying to keep up with her.

"There! Isn't this lovely? Is it far? I hope 'tis — I love to ride," sighed Pollyanna, as the wheels began to turn. "Of course, if 'tisn't far, I sha'n't mind, though, 'cause I'll be glad to get there all the sooner, you know. What a pretty street! I knew 'twas going to be pretty; father told me — "

She stopped with a little choking breath. Nancy, looking at her apprehensively, saw that her small chin was quivering, and that her eyes were full of tears. In a moment, however, she hurried on, with a brave lifting of her head.

"Father told me all about it. He remembered. And — and I ought to have explained before. Mrs. Gray told me to, at once — about this red gingham dress, you know, and why I'm not in black. She said you'd think 'twas queer. But there weren't any black things in the last missionary barrel, only

a lady's velvet basque which Deacon Carr's wife
said wasn't suitable for me at all; besides, it had
white spots — worn, you know — on both elbows,
and some other places. Part of the Ladies' Aid
wanted to buy me a black dress and hat, but the
other part thought the money ought to go toward
the red carpet they're trying to get — for the
church, you know. Mrs. White said maybe it was
just as well, anyway, for she didn't like children
in black — that is, I mean, she liked the children,
of course, but not the black part."

Pollyanna paused for breath, and Nancy managed
to stammer:

" Well, I'm sure it — it'll be all right."

" I'm glad you feel that way. I do, too," nodded
Pollyanna, again with that choking little breath.
" Of course, 'twould have been a good deal harder
to be glad in black — "

" Glad! " gasped Nancy, surprised into an inter-
ruption.

" Yes — that father's gone to Heaven to be with
mother and the rest of us, you know. He said I
must be glad. But it's been pretty hard to — to
do it, even in red gingham, because I — I wanted
him, so; and I couldn't help feeling I *ought* to have
him, specially as mother and the rest have God and

all the angels, while I didn't have anybody but the
Ladies' Aid. But now I'm sure it'll be easier because I've got you, Aunt Polly. I'm so glad I've
got you!"

Nancy's aching sympathy for the poor little for-
lornness beside her turned suddenly into shocked
terror.

"Oh, but — but you've made an awful mistake,
d-dear," she faltered. "I'm only Nancy. I ain't
your Aunt Polly, at all!"

"You — you *aren't?*" stammered the little girl,
in plain dismay.

"No. I'm only Nancy. I never thought of your
takin' me for her. We — we ain't a bit alike —
we ain't, we ain't!"

Timothy chuckled softly; but Nancy was too
disturbed to answer the merry flash from his eyes.

"But who *are* you?" questioned Pollyanna.
"You don't look a bit like a Ladies' Aider!"

Timothy laughed outright this time.

"I'm Nancy, the hired girl. I do all the work
except the washin' an' hard ironin'. Mis' Durgin
does that."

"But there *is* an Aunt Polly?" demanded the
child, anxiously.

"You bet your life there is," cut in Timothy.

Pollyanna relaxed visibly.

"Oh, that's all right, then." There was a moment's silence, then she went on brightly: "And do you know? I'm glad, after all, that she didn't come to meet me; because now I've got *her* still coming, and I've got you besides."

Nancy flushed. Timothy turned to her with a quizzical smile.

"I call that a pretty slick compliment," he said. "Why don't you thank the little lady?"

"I—I was thinkin' about—Miss Polly," faltered Nancy.

Pollyanna sighed contentedly.

"I was, too. I'm so interested in her. You know she's all the aunt I've got, and I didn't know I had her for ever so long. Then father told me. He said she lived in a lovely great big house 'way on top of a hill."

"She does. You can see it now," said Nancy. "It's that big white one with the green blinds, 'way ahead."

"Oh, how pretty!—and what a lot of trees and grass all around it! I never saw such a lot of green grass, seems so, all at once. Is my Aunt Polly rich, Nancy?"

"Yes, Miss."

" I'm so glad. It must be perfectly lovely to have lots of money. I never knew any one that did have, only the Whites — they're some rich. They have carpets in every room and ice-cream Sundays. Does Aunt Polly have ice-cream Sundays? "

Nancy shook her head. Her lips twitched. She threw a merry look into Timothy's eyes.

" No, Miss. Your aunt don't like ice-cream, I guess; leastways I never saw it on her table."

Pollyanna's face fell.

" Oh, doesn't she? I'm so sorry! I don't see how she can help liking ice-cream. But — anyhow, I can be kinder glad about that, 'cause the ice-cream you don't eat can't make your stomach ache like Mrs. White's did — that is, I ate hers, you know, lots of it. Maybe Aunt Polly has got the carpets, though."

" Yes, she's got the carpets."

" In every room? "

" Well, in almost every room," answered Nancy, frowning suddenly at the thought of that bare little attic room where there was no carpet.

" Oh, I'm so glad," exulted Pollyanna. " I love carpets. We didn't have any, only two little rugs that came in a missionary barrel, and one of those had ink spots on it. Mrs. White had pictures, too, perfectly beautiful ones of roses and little girls kneeling and a kitty and some lambs and a lion — not together, you know — the lambs and the lion. Oh, of course the Bible says they will sometime, but they haven't yet — that is, I mean Mrs. White's haven't. Don't you just love pictures?"

"I — I don't know," answered Nancy in a half-stifled voice.

"I do. We didn't have any pictures. They don't come in the barrels much, you know. There did two come once, though. But one was so good father sold it to get money to buy me some shoes with; and the other was so bad it fell to pieces just as soon as we hung it up. Glass — it broke, you know. And I cried. But I'm glad now we didn't have any of those nice things, 'cause I shall like Aunt Polly's all the better — not being used to 'em, you see. Just as it is when the *pretty* hair-ribbons come in the barrels after a lot of faded-out brown ones. My! but isn't this a perfectly beautiful house?" she broke off fervently, as they turned into the wide driveway.

It was when Timothy was unloading the trunk that Nancy found an opportunity to mutter low in his ear:

"Don't you never say nothin' ter me again about

leavin', Timothy Durgin. You couldn't *hire* me ter leave!"

"Leave! I should say not," grinned the youth. "You couldn't drag me away. It'll be more fun here now, with that kid 'round, than movin'-picture shows, every day!"

"Fun! — fun!" repeated Nancy, indignantly. "I guess it'll be somethin' more than fun for that blessed child — when them two tries ter live ter-gether; and I guess she'll be a-needin' some rock ter fly to for refuge. Well, I'm a-goin' ter be that rock, Timothy; I am, I am!" she vowed, as she turned and led Pollyanna up the broad steps.

CHAPTER IV

THE LITTLE ATTIC ROOM

MISS POLLY HARRINGTON did not rise to meet her niece. She looked up from her book, it is true, as Nancy and the little girl appeared in the sitting-room doorway, and she held out a hand with "duty" written large on every coldly extended finger.

"How do you do, Pollyanna? I—" She had no chance to say more. Pollyanna had fairly flown across the room and flung herself into her aunt's scandalized, unyielding lap.

"Oh, Aunt Polly, Aunt Polly, I don't know how to be glad enough that you let me come to live with you," she was sobbing. "You don't know how perfectly lovely it is to have you and Nancy and all this after you've had just the Ladies' Aid!"

"Very likely—though I've not had the pleasure of the Ladies' Aid's acquaintance," rejoined Miss Polly, stiffly, trying to unclasp the small, clinging fingers, and turning frowning eyes on Nancy in the doorway. "Nancy, that will do. You may go.

27

Pollyanna, be good enough, please, to stand erect in a proper manner. I don't know yet what you look like."

Pollyanna drew back at once, laughing a little hysterically.

" No, I suppose you don't; but you see I'm not very much to look at, anyway, on account of the freckles. Oh, and I ought to explain about the red gingham and the black velvet basque with white spots on the elbows. I told Nancy how father said —"

" Yes; well, never mind now what your father said," interrupted Miss Polly, crisply. " You had a trunk, I presume?"

" Oh, yes, indeed, Aunt Polly. I've got a beautiful trunk that the Ladies' Aid gave me. I haven't got so very much in it — of my own, I mean. The barrels haven't had many clothes for little girls in them lately; but there were all father's books, and Mrs. White said she thought I ought to have those. You see, father —"

" Pollyanna," interrupted her aunt again, sharply, " there is one thing that might just as well be understood right away at once; and that is, I do not care to have you keep talking of your father to me."

The little girl drew in her breath tremulously.

"Why, Aunt Polly, you — you mean — " She hesitated, and her aunt filled the pause.

"We will go up-stairs to your room. Your trunk is already there, I presume. I told Timothy to take it up — if you had one. You may follow me, Pollyanna."

Without speaking, Pollyanna turned and followed her aunt from the room. Her eyes were brimming with tears, but her chin was bravely high.

"After all, I — I reckon I'm glad she doesn't want me to talk about father," Pollyanna was thinking. "It'll be easier, maybe — if I don't talk about him. Probably, anyhow, that is why she told me not to talk about him." And Pollyanna, convinced anew of her aunt's "kindness," blinked off the tears and looked eagerly about her.

She was on the stairway now. Just ahead, her aunt's black silk skirt rustled luxuriously. Behind her an open door allowed a glimpse of soft-tinted rugs and satin-covered chairs. Beneath her feet a marvellous carpet was like green moss to the tread. On every side the gilt of picture frames or the glint of sunlight through the filmy mesh of lace curtains flashed in her eyes.

"Oh, Aunt Polly, Aunt Polly," breathed the little girl, rapturously; "what a perfectly lovely, lovely house! How awfully glad you must be you're so rich!"

"Polly*anna!*" ejaculated her aunt, turning sharply about as she reached the head of the stairs. "I'm surprised at you — making a speech like that to me!"

"Why, Aunt Polly, *aren't* you?" queried Polly-anna, in frank wonder.

"Certainly not, Pollyanna. I hope I could not so far forget myself as to be sinfully proud of any gift the Lord has seen fit to bestow upon me," declared the lady; "certainly not, of *riches!*"

Miss Polly turned and walked down the hall toward the attic stairway door. She was glad, now, that she had put the child in the attic room. Her idea at first had been to get her niece as far away as possible from herself, and at the same time place her where her childish heedlessness would not destroy valuable furnishings. Now — with this evident strain of vanity showing thus early — it was all the more fortunate that the room planned for her was plain and sensible, thought Miss Polly.

Eagerly Pollyanna's small feet pattered behind

her aunt. Still more eagerly her big blue eyes tried
to look in all directions at once, that no thing of
beauty or interest in this wonderful house might
be passed unseen. Most eagerly of all her mind
turned to the wondrously exciting problem about to
be solved: behind which of all these fascinating
doors was waiting now her room — the dear, beautiful room full of curtains, rugs, and pictures, that
was to be her very own? Then, abruptly, her
aunt opened a door and ascended another stairway.

There was little to be seen here. A bare wall
rose on either side. At the top of the stairs, wide
reaches of shadowy space led to far corners where
the roof came almost down to the floor, and where
were stacked innumerable trunks and boxes. It was
hot and stifling, too. Unconsciously Pollyanna
lifted her head higher — it seemed so hard to
breathe. Then she saw that her aunt had thrown
open a door at the right.

" There, Pollyanna, here is your room, and your
trunk is here, I see. Have you your key? "

Pollyanna nodded dumbly. Her eyes were a
little wide and frightened.

Her aunt frowned.

" When I ask a question, Pollyanna, I prefer that

you should answer aloud — not merely with your head."

" Yes, Aunt Polly."

" Thank you; that is better. I believe you have everything that you need here," she added, glancing at the well-filled towel rack and water pitcher. " I will send Nancy up to help you unpack. Supper is at six o'clock," she finished, as she left the room and swept down-stairs.

For a moment after she had gone Pollyanna stood quite still, looking after her. Then she turned her wide eyes to the bare wall, the bare floor, the bare windows. She turned them last to the little trunk that had stood not so long before in her own little room in the far-away Western home. The next moment she stumbled blindly toward it and fell on her knees at its side, covering her face with her hands.

Nancy found her there when she came up a few minutes later.

" There, there, you poor lamb," she crooned, dropping to the floor and drawing the little girl into her arms. " I was just a-fearin' I'd find you like this, like this."

Pollyanna shook her head.

" But I'm bad and wicked, Nancy — awful

wicked," she sobbed. "I just can't make myself understand that God and the angels needed my father more than I did."

"No more they did, neither," declared Nancy, stoutly.

"Oh-h!—*Nancy!*" The burning horror in Pollyanna's eyes dried the tears.

Nancy gave a shamefaced smile and rubbed her own eyes vigorously.

"There, there, child, I didn't mean it, of course," she cried briskly. "Come, let's have your key and we'll get inside this trunk and take our your dresses in no time, no time."

Somewhat tearfully Pollyanna produced the key.

"There aren't very many there, anyway," she faltered.

"Then they're all the sooner unpacked," declared Nancy.

Pollyanna gave a sudden radiant smile.

"That's so! I can be glad of that, can't I?" she cried.

Nancy stared.

"Why, of — course," she answered a little uncertainly.

Nancy's capable hands made short work of unpacking the books, the patched undergarments, and the few pitifully unattractive dresses. Pollyanna, smiling bravely now, flew about, hanging the dresses in the closet, stacking the books on the table, and putting away the undergarments in the bureau drawers.

" I'm sure it — it's going to be a very nice room. Don't you think so? " she stammered, after a while.

There was no answer. Nancy was very busy, apparently, with her head in the trunk. Pollyanna, standing at the bureau, gazed a little wistfully at the bare wall above.

" And I can be glad there isn't any looking-glass here, too, 'cause where there *isn't* any glass I can't see my freckles."

Nancy made a sudden queer little sound with her mouth — but when Pollyanna turned, her head was in the trunk again. At one of the windows, a few minutes later, Pollyanna gave a glad cry and clapped her hands joyously.

" Oh, Nancy, I hadn't seen this before," she breathed. " Look — 'way off there, with those trees and the houses and that lovely church spire, and the river shining just like silver. Why, Nancy, there doesn't anybody need any pictures with that to look at. Oh, I'm so glad now she let me have this room!"

To Pollyanna's surprise and dismay, Nancy burst into tears. Pollyanna hurriedly crossed to her side.

" Why, Nancy, Nancy — what is it? " she cried; then, fearfully: " This wasn't — *your* room, was it? "

" My room! " stormed Nancy, hotly, choking back the tears. " If you ain't a little angel straight from Heaven, and if some folks don't eat dirt before — Oh, land! there's her bell! " After which amazing speech, Nancy sprang to her feet, dashed out of the room, and went clattering down the stairs.

Left alone, Pollyanna went back to her " picture," as she mentally designated the beautiful view from the window. After a time she touched the sash tentatively. It seemed as if no longer could she endure the stifling heat. To her joy the sash moved under her fingers. The next moment the window was wide open, and Pollyanna was leaning far out, drinking in the fresh, sweet air.

She ran then to the other window. That, too, soon flew up under her eager hands. A big fly swept past her nose, and buzzed noisily about the room. Then another came, and another; but Pollyanna paid no heed. Pollyanna had made a wonderful discovery — against this window a huge tree flung great branches. To Pollyanna they looked like arms outstretched, inviting her.

Suddenly she laughed aloud.

" I believe I can do it," she chuckled. The next moment she had climbed nimbly to the window ledge. From there it was an easy matter to step to the nearest tree-branch. Then, clinging like a monkey, she swung herself from limb to limb until the lowest branch was reached. The drop to the ground was — even for Pollyanna, who was used to climbing trees — a little fearsome. She took it, however, with bated breath, swinging from her strong little arms, and landing on all fours in the soft grass. Then she picked herself up and looked eagerly about her.

She was at the back of the house. Before her lay a garden in which a bent old man was working. Beyond the garden a little path through an open field led up a steep hill, at the top of which a lone pine tree stood on guard beside the huge rock. To Pollyanna, at the moment, there seemed to be just one place in the world worth being in — the top of that big rock.

With a run and a skilful turn, Pollyanna skipped by the bent old man, threaded her way between the orderly rows of green growing things, and — a little out of breath — reached the path that ran through the open field. Then, determinedly, she began to climb. Already, however, she was thinking what a long, long way off that rock must be, when back at the window it had looked so near!

Fifteen minutes later the great clock in the hall-way of the Harrington homestead struck six. At precisely the last stroke Nancy sounded the bell for supper.

One, two, three minutes passed. Miss Polly frowned and tapped the floor with her slipper. A little jerkily she rose to her feet, went into the hall, and looked up-stairs, plainly impatient. For a minute she listened intently; then she turned and swept into the dining room.

"Nancy," she said with decision, as soon as the little serving-maid appeared; "my niece is late. No, you need not call her," she added severely, as Nancy made a move toward the hall door. "I told her what time supper was, and now she will have to suffer the consequences. She may as well begin at once to learn to be punctual. When she comes down she may have bread and milk in the kitchen."

"Yes, ma'am." It was well, perhaps, that Miss

Polly did not happen to be looking at Nancy's face just then.

At the earliest possible moment after supper, Nancy crept up the back stairs and thence to the attic room.

"Bread and milk, indeed! — and when the poor lamb hain't only just cried herself to sleep," she was muttering fiercely, as she softly pushed open the door. The next moment she gave a frightened cry. "Where are you? Where've you gone? Where *have* you gone?" she panted, looking in the closet, under the bed, and even in the trunk and down the water pitcher. Then she flew down-stairs and out to Old Tom in the garden.

"Mr. Tom, Mr. Tom, that blessed child's gone," she wailed. "She's vanished right up into Heaven where she come from, poor lamb — and me told ter give her bread and milk in the kitchen — her what's eatin' angel food this minute, I'll warrant, I'll warrant!"

The old man straightened up.

"Gone? Heaven?" he repeated stupidly, unconsciously sweeping the brilliant sunset sky with his gaze. He stopped, stared a moment intently, then turned with a slow grin. "Well, Nancy, it do look like as if she'd tried ter get as nigh Heaven as she could, and that's a fact," he agreed, pointing with a crooked finger to where, sharply outlined against the reddening sky, a slender, wind-blown figure was poised on top of a huge rock.

"Well, she ain't goin' ter Heaven that way ter-night — not if I has my say," declared Nancy, doggedly. "If the mistress asks, tell her I ain't furgettin' the dishes, but I gone on a stroll," she flung back over her shoulder, as she sped toward the path that led through the open field.

CHAPTER V

THE GAME

"For the land's sake, Miss Pollyanna, what a scare you did give me," panted Nancy, hurrying up to the big rock, down which Pollyanna had just regretfully slid.

"Scare? Oh, I'm so sorry; but you mustn't, really, ever get scared about me, Nancy. Father and the Ladies' Aid used to do it, too, till they found I always came back all right."

"But I didn't even know you'd went," cried Nancy, tucking the little girl's hand under her arm and hurrying her down the hill. "I didn't see you go, and nobody didn't. I guess you flew right up through the roof; I do, I do."

Pollyanna skipped gleefully.

"I did, 'most — only I flew down instead of up. I came down the tree."

Nancy stopped short.

"You did — what?"

"Came down the tree, outside my window."

" My stars and stockings!" gasped Nancy, hurrying on again. " I'd like ter know what yer aunt
would say ter that!"

"Would you? Well, I'll tell her, then, so
you can find out," promised the little girl, cheerfully.

" Mercy!" gasped Nancy. " No — no!"

"Why, you don't mean she'd *care!*" cried
Pollyanna, plainly disturbed.

" No — er — yes — well, never mind. I — I
ain't so very particular about knowin' what she'd
say, truly," stammered Nancy, determined to keep
one scolding from Pollyanna, if nothing more.
" But, say, we better hurry. I've got ter get them
dishes done, ye know."

" I'll help," promised Pollyanna, promptly.

"Oh, Miss Pollyanna!" demurred Nancy.

For a moment there was silence. The sky was
darkening fast. Pollyanna took a firmer hold of her
friend's arm.

" I reckon I'm glad, after all, that you *did* get
scared — a little, 'cause then you came after me,"
she shivered.

" Poor little lamb! And you must be hungry,
too. I — I'm afraid you'll have ter have bread and
milk in the kitchen with me. Yer aunt didn't like

it — because you didn't come down ter supper, ye know."

" But I couldn't. I was up here."

" Yes; but — she didn't know that, you see," observed Nancy, dryly, stifling a chuckle. " I'm sorry about the bread and milk; I am, I am."

" Oh, I'm not. I'm glad."

" Glad! Why? "

" Why, I like bread and milk, and I'd like to eat with you. I don't see any trouble about being glad about that."

" You don't seem ter see any trouble bein' glad about everythin'," retorted Nancy, choking a little over her remembrance of Pollyanna's brave attempts to like the bare little attic room.

Pollyanna laughed softly.

" Well, that's the game, you know, anyway."

" The — *game?* "

" Yes; the ' just being glad ' game."

" Whatever in the world are you talkin' about? "

" Why, it's a game. Father told it to me, and it's lovely," rejoined Pollyanna. " We've played it always, ever since I was a little, little girl. I told the Ladies' Aid, and they played it — some of them."

" What is it? I ain't much on games, though."

Pollyanna laughed again, but she sighed, too; and in the gathering twilight her face looked thin and wistful.

"Why, we began it on some crutches that came in a missionary barrel."

"*Crutches!*"

"Yes. You see I'd wanted a doll, and father had written them so; but when the barrel came the lady wrote that there hadn't any dolls come in, but the little crutches had. So she sent 'em along as they might come in handy for some child, sometime. And that's when we began it."

"Well, I must say I can't see any game about that, about that," declared Nancy, almost irritably.

"Oh, yes; the game was to just find something about everything to be glad about — no matter what 'twas," rejoined Pollyanna, earnestly. "And we began right then — on the crutches."

"Well, goodness me! I can't see anythin' ter be glad about — gettin' a pair of crutches when you wanted a doll!"

Pollyanna clapped her hands.

"There is — there is," she crowed. "But *I* couldn't see it, either, Nancy, at first," she added, with quick honesty. "Father had to tell it to me."

"Well, then, suppose *you* tell *me*," almost snapped Nancy.

"Goosey! Why, just be glad because you *don't* — *need* — *'em!*" exulted Pollyanna, triumphantly. "You see it's just as easy — when you know how!"

"Well, of all the queer doin's!" breathed Nancy, regarding Pollyanna with almost fearful eyes.

"Oh, but it isn't queer — it's lovely," maintained Pollyanna enthusiastically. "And we've played it ever since. And the harder 'tis, the more fun 'tis to get 'em out; only — only — sometimes it's almost too hard — like when your father goes to Heaven, and there isn't anybody but a Ladies' Aid left."

"Yes, or when you're put in a snippy little room 'way at the top of the house with nothin' in it," growled Nancy.

Pollyanna sighed.

"That *was* a hard one, at first," she admitted, "specially when I was so kind of lonesome. I just didn't feel like playing the game, anyway, and I *had* been wanting pretty things, so! Then I happened to think how I hated to see my freckles in the looking-glass, and I saw that lovely picture out the window, too; so then I knew I'd found the things to be glad about. You see, when you're hunting for the glad things, you sort of forget the other kind — like the doll you wanted, you know."

"Humph!" choked Nancy, trying to swallow the lump in her throat.

"Most generally it doesn't take so long," sighed Pollyanna; "and lots of times now I just think of them *without* thinking, you know. I've got so used to playing it. It's a lovely game. F-father and I used to like it so much," she faltered. "I suppose, though, it — it'll be a little harder now, as long as I haven't anybody to play it with. Maybe Aunt Polly will play it, though," she added, as an afterthought.

"My stars and stockings! — *her!*" breathed Nancy, behind her teeth. Then, aloud, she said doggedly: "See here, Miss Pollyanna, I ain't sayin' that I'll play it very well, and I ain't sayin' that I know how, anyway; but I'll play it with ye, after a fashion — I just will, I will!"

."Oh, Nancy!" exulted Pollyanna, giving her a rapturous hug. "That'll be splendid! Won't we have fun?"

"Er — maybe," conceded Nancy, in open doubt. "But you mustn't count too much on me, ye know. I never was no case fur games, but I'm a-goin' ter make a most awful old try on this one. You're goin' ter have some one ter play it with, anyhow," she finished, as they entered the kitchen together.

Pollyanna ate her bread and milk with good appetite; then, at Nancy's suggestion, she went into the sitting room, where her aunt sat reading.

Miss Polly looked up coldly.

" Have you had your supper, Pollyanna? "

" Yes, Aunt Polly."

" I'm very sorry, Pollyanna, to have been obliged so soon to send you into the kitchen to eat bread and milk."

" But I was real glad you did it, Aunt Polly. I like bread and milk, and Nancy, too. You mustn't feel bad about that one bit."

Aunt Polly sat suddenly a little more erect in her chair.

" Pollyanna, it's quite time you were in bed. You have had a hard day, and to-morrow we must plan your hours and go over your clothing to see what it is necessary to get for you. Nancy will give you a candle. Be careful how you handle it. Breakfast will be at half-past seven. See that you are down to that. Good-night."

Quite as a matter of course, Pollyanna came

straight to her aunt's side and gave her an affectionate hug.

"I've had such a beautiful time, so far," she sighed happily. "I know I'm going to just love living with you — but then, I knew I should before I came. Good-night," she called cheerfully, as she ran from the room.

"Well, upon my soul!" ejaculated Miss Polly, half aloud. "What a most extraordinary child!" Then she frowned. "She's 'glad' I punished her, and I 'mustn't feel bad one bit,' and she's going to 'love to live' with me! Well, upon my soul!" ejaculated Miss Polly again, as she took up her book.

Fifteen minutes later, in the attic room, a lonely little girl sobbed into the tightly-clutched sheet:

"I know, father-among-the-angels, I'm not playing the game one bit now — not one bit; but I don't believe even you could find anything to be glad about sleeping all alone 'way off up here in the dark — like this. If only I was near Nancy or Aunt Polly, or even a Ladies' Aider, it would be easier!"

Down-stairs in the kitchen, Nancy, hurrying with her belated work, jabbed her dish-mop into the milk pitcher, and muttered jerkily:

" If playin' a silly-fool game — about bein' glad you've got crutches when you want dolls — is got ter be — my way — o' bein' that rock o' refuge — why, I'm a-goin' ter play it — I am, I am! "

CHAPTER VI

A QUESTION OF DUTY

It was nearly seven o'clock when Pollyanna awoke that first day after her arrival. Her windows faced the south and the west, so she could not see the sun yet; but she could see the hazy blue of the morning sky, and she knew that the day promised to be a fair one.

The little room was cooler now, and the air blew in fresh and sweet. Outside, the birds were twittering joyously, and Pollyanna flew to the window to talk to them. She saw then that down in the garden her aunt was already out among the rose-bushes. With rapid fingers, therefore, she made herself ready to join her.

Down the attic stairs sped Pollyanna, leaving both doors wide open. Through the hall, down the next flight, then bang through the front screened-door and around to the garden, she ran.

Aunt Polly, with the bent old man, was leaning over a rose-bush when Pollyanna, gurgling with delight, flung herself upon her.

" Oh, Aunt Polly, Aunt Polly, I reckon I am glad this morning just to be alive ! "

" Poll*yanna !* " remonstrated the lady, sternly, pulling herself as erect as she could with a dragging weight of ninety pounds hanging about her neck. " Is this the usual way you say good morning ? "

The little girl dropped to her toes, and danced lightly up and down.

" No, only when I love folks so I just can't help it ! I saw you from my window, Aunt Polly, and I got to thinking how you *weren't* a Ladies' Aider, and you were my really truly aunt; and you looked so good I just had to come down and hug you ! "

The bent old man turned his back suddenly. Miss Polly attempted a frown — with not her usual success.

" Pollyanna, you — I — Thomas, that will do for this morning. I think you understand — about those rose-bushes," she said stiffly. Then she turned and walked rapidly away.

" Do you always work in the garden, Mr. — Man ? " asked Pollyanna, interestedly.

The man turned. His lips were twitching, but his eyes looked blurred as if with tears.

" Yes, Miss. I'm Old Tom, the gardener," he

answered. Timidly, but as if impelled by an irresistible force, he reached out a shaking hand and let it rest for a moment on her bright hair. " You are so like your mother, little Miss! I used ter know her when she was even littler than you be. You see, I used ter work in the garden — then."

Pollyanna caught her breath audibly.

" You did? And you knew my mother, really — when she was just a little earth angel, and not a Heaven one? Oh, please tell me about her! " And down plumped Pollyanna in the middle of the dirt path by the old man's side.

A bell sounded from the house. The next moment Nancy was seen flying out the back door.

" Miss Pollyanna, that bell means breakfast — mornin's," she panted, pulling the little girl to her feet and hurrying her back to the house; " and other times it means other meals. But it always means that you're ter run like time when ye hear it, no matter where ye be. If ye don't — well, it'll take somethin' smarter'n we be ter find *anythin'* ter be glad about in that! " she finished, shooing Pollyanna into the house as she would shoo an unruly chicken into a coop.

Breakfast, for the first five minutes, was a silent meal; then Miss Polly, her disapproving eyes following the airy wings of two flies darting here and there over the table, said sternly:

"Nancy, where did those flies come from?"

"I don't know, ma'am. There wasn't one in the kitchen." Nancy had been too excited to notice Pollyanna's up-flung windows the afternoon before.

"I reckon maybe they're my flies, Aunt Polly," observed Pollyanna, amiably. "There were lots of them this morning having a beautiful time upstairs."

Nancy left the room precipitately, though to do so she had to carry out the hot muffins she had just brought in.

"Yours!" gasped Miss Polly. "What do you mean? Where did they come from?"

"Why, Aunt Polly, they came from out of doors, of course, through the windows. I *saw* some of them come in."

"You saw them! You mean you raised those windows without any screens?"

"Why, yes. There weren't any screens there, Aunt Polly."

Nancy, at this moment, came in again with the muffins. Her face was grave, but very red.

"Nancy," directed her mistress, sharply, "you may set the muffins down and go at once to Miss

Pollyanna's room and shut the windows. Shut the doors, also. Later, when your morning work is done, go through every room with the spatter. See that you make a thorough search."

To her niece she said:

" Pollyanna, I have ordered screens for those windows. I knew, of course, that it was my duty to do that. But it seems to me that you have quite forgotten *your* duty."

" My — duty? " Pollyanna's eyes were wide with wonder.

"Certainly. I know it is warm, but I consider it your duty to keep your windows closed till those screens come. Flies, Pollyanna, are not only unclean and annoying, but very dangerous to health. After breakfast I will give you a little pamphlet on this matter to read."

" To read? Oh, thank you, Aunt Polly. I love to read! "

Miss Polly drew in her breath audibly, then she shut her lips together hard. Pollyanna, seeing her stern face, frowned a little thoughtfully.

" Of course I'm sorry about the duty I forgot, Aunt Polly," she apologized timidly. " I won't raise the windows again."

Her aunt made no reply. She did not speak, in-

deed, until the meal was over. Then she rose, went
to the bookcase in the sitting room, took out a small
paper booklet, and crossed the room to her niece's
side.

"This is the article I spoke of, Pollyanna. I desire you to go to your room at once and read it. I
will be up in half an hour to look over your things."

Pollyanna, her eyes on the illustration of a fly's
head, many times magnified, cried joyously:

"Oh, thank you, Aunt Polly!" The next moment she skipped merrily from the room, banging
the door behind her.

Miss Polly frowned, hesitated, then crossed the
room majestically and opened the door; but Pollyanna was already out of sight, clattering up the
attic stairs.

Half an hour later when Miss Polly, her face ex-
pressing stern duty in every line, climbed those
stairs and entered Pollyanna's room, she was
greeted with a burst of eager enthusiasm.

"Oh, Aunt Polly, I never saw anything so perfectly lovely and interesting in my life. I'm so glad
you gave me that book to read! Why, I didn't
suppose flies could carry such a lot of things on
their feet, and — "

"That will do," observed Aunt Polly, with dignity. " Pollyanna, you may bring out your clothes now, and I will look them over. What are not suitable for you I shall give to the Sullivans, of course."

With visible reluctance Pollyanna laid down the pamphlet and turned toward the closet.

" I'm afraid you'll think they're worse than the Ladies' Aid did — and *they* said they were shameful," she sighed. " But there were mostly things for boys and older folks in the last two or three barrels; and — did you ever have a missionary barrel, Aunt Polly?"

At her aunt's look of shocked anger, Pollyanna corrected herself at once.

" Why, no, of course you didn't, Aunt Polly!" she hurried on, with a hot blush. " I forgot; rich folks never have to have them. But you see sometimes I kind of forget that you *are* rich — up here in this room, you know."

Miss Polly's lips parted indignantly, but no words came. Pollyanna, plainly unaware that she had said anything in the least unpleasant, was hurrying on.

" Well, as I was going to say, you can't tell a thing about missionary barrels — except that you won't find in 'em what you think you're going to — even when you think you won't. It was the barrels every time, too, that were hardest to play the game on, for father and — ”

Just in time Pollyanna remembered that she was not to talk of her father to her aunt. She dived into her closet then, hurriedly, and brought out all the poor little dresses in both her arms.

“ They aren’t nice, at all,” she choked, “ and they’d been black if it hadn’t been for the red carpet for the church; but they’re all I’ve got.”

With the tips of her fingers Miss Polly turned over the conglomerate garments, so obviously made for anybody but Pollyanna. Next she bestowed frowning attention on the patched undergarments in the bureau drawers.

“ I’ve got the best ones on,” confessed Polly-anna, anxiously. “ The Ladies’ Aid bought me one set straight through all whole. Mrs. Jones — she’s the president — told ’em I should have that if they had to clatter down bare aisles themselves the rest of their days. But they won’t. Mr. White doesn’t like the noise. He’s got nerves, his wife says; but he’s got money, too, and they expect he’ll give a lot toward the carpet — on account of the nerves, you know. I should think he’d be glad that if he did have the nerves he’d got money, too; shouldn’t you? ”

Miss Polly did not seem to hear. Her scrutiny of the undergarments finished, she turned to Pollyanna somewhat abruptly.

"You have been to school, of course, Pollyanna?"

"Oh, yes, Aunt Polly. Besides, fath— I mean, I was taught at home some, too."

Miss Polly frowned.

"Very good. In the fall you will enter school here, of course. Mr. Hall, the principal, will doubtless settle in which grade you belong. Meanwhile, I suppose I ought to hear you read aloud half an hour each day."

"I love to read; but if you don't want to hear me I'd be just glad to read to myself — truly, Aunt Polly. And I wouldn't have to half try to be glad, either, for I like best to read to myself — on account of the big words, you know."

"I don't doubt it," rejoined Miss Polly, grimly. "Have you studied music?"

"Not much. I don't like my music — I like other people's, though. I learned to play on the piano a little. Miss Gray — she plays for church — she taught me. But I'd just as soon let that go as not, Aunt Polly. I'd rather, truly."

" Very likely," observed Aunt Polly, with slightly uplifted eyebrows. " Nevertheless I think it is my duty to see that you are properly instructed in at least the rudiments of music. You sew, of course."

" Yes, ma'am." Pollyanna sighed. " The Ladies' Aid taught me that. But I had an awful time. Mrs. Jones didn't believe in holding your needle like the rest of 'em did on buttonholing, and Mrs. White thought backstitching ought to be taught you before hemming (or else the other way), and Mrs. Harriman didn't believe in putting you on patchwork ever, at all."

" Well, there will be no difficulty of that kind any longer, Pollyanna. I shall teach you sewing myself, of course. You do not know how to cook, I presume."

Pollyanna laughed suddenly.

· " They were just beginning to teach me that this summer, but I hadn't got far. They were more divided up on that than they were on the sewing. They were *going* to begin on bread; but there wasn't two of 'em that made it alike, so after arguing it all one sewing-meeting, they decided to take turns at me one forenoon a week — in their own kitchens, you know. I'd only learned chocolate fudge and fig cake, though, when — when I had to stop." Her voice broke.

"Chocolate fudge and fig cake, indeed!" scorned Miss Polly. "I think we can remedy that very soon." She paused in thought for a minute, then went on slowly: "At nine o'clock every morning you will read aloud one half-hour to me. Before that you will use the time to put this room in order. Wednesday and Saturday forenoons, after half-past nine, you will spend with Nancy in the kitchen, learning to cook. Other mornings you will sew with me. That will leave the afternoons for your music. I shall, of course, procure a teacher at once for you," she finished decisively, as she arose from her chair.

Pollyanna cried out in dismay.

"Oh, but Aunt Polly, Aunt Polly, you haven't left me any time at all just to — to live."

"To live, child! What do you mean? As if you weren't living all the time!"

"Oh, of course I'd be *breathing* all the time I was doing those things, Aunt Polly, but I wouldn't be living. You breathe all the time you're asleep, but you aren't living. I mean *living* — doing the things you want to do: playing outdoors, reading (to myself, of course), climbing hills, talking to Mr.

Tom in the garden, and Nancy, and finding out all about the houses and the people and everything everywhere all through the perfectly lovely streets I came through yesterday. That's what I call living, Aunt Polly. Just breathing isn't living!"

Miss Polly lifted her head irritably.

"Pollyanna, you *are* the most extraordinary child! You will be allowed a proper amount of playtime, of course. But, surely, it seems to me if I am willing to do my duty in seeing that you have proper care and instruction, *you* ought to be willing to do yours by seeing that that care and instruction are not ungratefully wasted."

Pollyanna looked shocked.

"Oh, Aunt Polly, as if I ever could be ungrateful — to *you!* Why, I *love* you — and you aren't even a Ladies' Aider; you're an aunt!"

"Very well; then see that you don't act ungrateful," vouchsafed Miss Polly, as she turned toward the door.

She had gone halfway down the stairs when a small, unsteady voice called after her:

"Please, Aunt Polly, you didn't tell me which of my things you wanted to — to give away."

Aunt Polly emitted a tired sigh — a sigh that ascended straight to Pollyanna's ears.

"Oh, I forgot to tell you, Pollyanna. Timothy will drive us into town at half-past one this afternoon. Not one of your garments is fit for my niece to wear. Certainly I should be very far from doing my duty by you if I should let you appear out in any one of them."

Pollyanna sighed now — she believed she was going to hate that word — duty.

"Aunt Polly, please," she called wistfully, "isn't there *any* way you can be glad about all that — duty business?"

"What?" Miss Polly looked up in dazed surprise; then, suddenly, with very red cheeks, she turned and swept angrily down the stairs. "Don't be impertinent, Pollyanna!"

In the hot little attic room Pollyanna dropped herself on to one of the straight-backed chairs. To her, existence loomed ahead one endless round of duty.

"I don't see, really, what there was impertinent about that," she sighed. "I was only asking her if she couldn't tell me something to be glad about in all that duty business."

For several minutes Pollyanna sat in silence, her

rueful eyes fixed on the forlorn heap of garments on the bed. Then, slowly, she rose and began to put away the dresses.

" There just isn't anything to be glad about, that I can see," she said aloud; " unless — it's to be glad when the duty's done!" Whereupon she laughed suddenly.

CHAPTER VII

POLLYANNA AND PUNISHMENTS

AT half-past one o'clock Timothy drove Miss Polly and her niece to the four or five principal dry goods stores, which were about half a mile from the homestead.

Fitting Pollyanna with a new wardrobe proved to be more or less of an exciting experience for all concerned. Miss Polly came out of it with the feeling of limp relaxation that one might have at finding oneself at last on solid earth after a perilous walk across the very thin crust of a volcano. The various clerks who had waited upon the pair came out of it with very red faces, and enough amusing stories of Pollyanna to keep their friends in gales of laughter the rest of the week. Pollyanna herself came out of it with radiant smiles and a heart content; for, as she expressed it to one of the clerks: "When you haven't had anybody but missionary barrels and Ladies' Aiders to dress you, it *is* perfectly lovely to just walk right in and buy clothes that are brand-new, and that don't have to be tucked up or let down because they don't fit!"

The shopping expedition consumed the entire afternoon; then came supper and a delightful talk with Old Tom in the garden, and another with Nancy on the back porch, after the dishes were done, and while Aunt Polly paid a visit to a neighbor.

Old Tom told Pollyanna wonderful things of her mother, that made her very happy indeed; and Nancy told her all about the little farm six miles away at "The Corners," where lived her own dear mother, and her equally dear brother and sisters. She promised, too, that sometime, if Miss Polly were willing, Pollyanna should be taken to see them.

"And *they've* got lovely names, too. You'll like *their* names," sighed Nancy. "They're ' Algernon,' and ' Florabelle ' and ' Estelle.' I — I just hate ' Nancy '! "

"Oh, Nancy, what a dreadful thing to say! Why?"

"Because it isn't pretty like the others. You see, I was the first baby, and mother hadn't begun ter read so many stories with the pretty names in 'em, then."

"But I love ' Nancy,' just because it's you," declared Pollyanna.

" Humph! Well, I guess you could love ' Clarissa Mabelle ' just as well," retorted Nancy, " and it would be a heap happier for me. I think *that* name's just grand! "

Pollyanna laughed.

" Well, anyhow," she chuckled, " you can be glad it isn't ' Hephzibah.' "

" Hephzibah! "

" Yes. Mrs. White's name is that. Her husband calls her ' Hep,' and she doesn't like it. She says when he calls out ' Hep — Hep!' she feels just as if the next minute he was going to yell ' Hurrah!' And she doesn't like to be hurrahed at."

Nancy's gloomy face relaxed into a broad smile.

" Well, if you don't beat the Dutch! Say, do you know? — I sha'n't never hear ' Nancy ' now that I don't think o' that ' Hep — Hep!' and giggle. My, I guess I *am* glad — " She stopped short and turned amazed eyes on the little girl. " Say, Miss Pollyanna, do you mean — was you playin' that 'ere game *then* — about my bein' glad I wa'n't named ' Hephzibah '? "

Pollyanna frowned; then she laughed.

" Why, Nancy, that's so! I *was* playing the game — but that's one of the times I just did it without thinking, I reckon. You see, you *do,* lots of times:

you get so used to it — looking for something to be glad about, you know. And most generally there *is* something about everything that you can be glad about, if you keep hunting long enough to find it."

" Well, m-maybe," granted Nancy, with open doubt.

At half-past eight Pollyanna went up to bed. The screens had not yet come, and the close little room was like an oven. With longing eyes Pollyanna looked at the two fast-closed windows — but she did not raise them. She undressed, folded her clothes neatly, said her prayers, blew out her candle and climbed into bed.

Just how long she lay in sleepless misery, tossing from side to side of the hot little cot, she did not know; but it seemed to her that it must have been hours before she finally slipped out of bed, felt her way across the room and opened her door.

Out in the main attic all was velvet blackness save where the moon flung a path of silver half-way across the floor from the east dormer window. With a resolute ignoring of that fearsome darkness to the right and to the left, Pollyanna drew a quick breath and pattered straight into that silvery path, and on to the window.

She had hoped, vaguely, that this window might have a screen, but it did not. Outside, however, there was a wide world of fairy-like beauty, and there was, too, she knew, fresh, sweet air that would feel so good to hot cheeks and hands!

As she stepped nearer and peered longingly out, she saw something else: she saw, only a little way below the window, the wide, flat tin roof of Miss Polly's sun parlor built over the porte-cochère. The sight filled her with longing. If only, now, she were out there!

Fearfully she looked behind her. Back there, somewhere, were her hot little room and her still hotter bed; but between her and them lay a horrid desert of blackness across which one must feel one's way with outstretched, shrinking arms; while before her, out on the sun-parlor roof, were the moonlight and the cool, sweet night air.

If only her bed were out there! And folks did sleep out of doors. Joel Hartley at home, who was so sick with the consumption, *had* to sleep out of doors.

Suddenly Pollyanna remembered that she had seen near this attic window a row of long white bags hanging from nails. Nancy had said that they contained the winter clothing, put away for the summer. A little fearfully now, Pollyanna felt her way to these bags, selected a nice fat soft one (it contained Miss Polly's sealskin coat) for a bed; and a thinner one to be doubled up for a pillow, and still another (which was so thin it seemed almost empty) for a covering. Thus equipped, Pollyanna in high glee pattered to the moonlit window again, raised the sash, stuffed her burden through to the roof below, then let herself down after it, closing the window carefully behind her — Pollyanna had not forgotten those flies with the marvellous feet that carried things.

How deliciously cool it was! Pollyanna quite danced up and down with delight, drawing in long, full breaths of the refreshing air. The tin roof under her feet crackled with little resounding snaps that Pollyanna rather liked. She walked, indeed, two or three times back and forth from end to end — it gave her such a pleasant sensation of airy space after her hot little room; and the roof was so broad and flat that she had no fear of falling off. Finally, with a sigh of content, she curled herself up on the sealskin-coat mattress, arranged one bag for a pillow and the other for a covering, and settled herself to sleep.

"I'm so glad now that the screens didn't come,"

she murmured, blinking up at the stars; "else I couldn't have had this!"

Down-stairs in Miss Polly's room next the sun parlor, Miss Polly herself was hurrying into dressing gown and slippers, her face white and frightened. A minute before she had been telephoning in a shaking voice to Timothy:

"Come up quick! — you and your father. Bring lanterns. Somebody is on the roof of the sun parlor. He must have climbed up the rose-trellis or somewhere, and of course he can get right into the house through the east window in the attic. I have locked the attic door down here — but hurry, quick!"

Some time later, Pollyanna, just dropping off to sleep, was startled by a lantern flash, and a trio of amazed ejaculations. She opened her eyes to find Timothy at the top of a ladder near her, Old Tom just getting through the window, and her aunt peering out at her from behind him.

"Pollyanna, what does this mean?" cried Aunt Polly then.

Pollyanna blinked sleepy eyes and sat up.

"Why, Mr. Tom — Aunt Polly!" she stammered. "Don't look so scared! It isn't that I've got the consumption, you know, like Joel Hartley.

It's only that I was so hot — in there. But I shut the window, Aunt Polly, so the flies couldn't carry those germ-things in."

Timothy disappeared suddenly down the ladder. Old Tom, with almost equal precipitation, handed his lantern to Miss Polly, and followed his son. Miss Polly bit her lip hard — until the men were gone; then she said sternly:

" Pollyanna, hand those things to me at once and come in here. Of all the extraordinary children! " she ejaculated a little later, as, with Pollyanna by her side, and the lantern in her hand, she turned back into the attic.

To Pollyanna the air was all the more stifling after that cool breath of the out of doors; but she did not complain. She only drew a long quivering sigh.

At the top of the stairs Miss Polly jerked out crisply:

" For the rest of the night, Pollyanna, you are to sleep in my bed with me. The screens will be here to-morrow, but until then I consider it my duty to keep you where I know where you are."

Pollyanna drew in her breath.

" With you? — in your bed? " she cried rapturously. " Oh, Aunt Polly, Aunt Polly, how perfectly lovely of you! And when I've so wanted to sleep with some one sometime — some one that belonged to me, you know; not a Ladies' Aider. I've *had* them. My! I reckon I am glad now those screens didn't come! Wouldn't you be?"

There was no reply. Miss Polly was stalking on ahead. Miss Polly, to tell the truth, was feeling curiously helpless. For the third time since Pollyanna's arrival, Miss Polly was punishing Pollyanna — and for the third time she was being confronted with the amazing fact that her punishment was being taken as a special reward of merit. No wonder Miss Polly was feeling curiously helpless.

CHAPTER VIII

POLLYANNA PAYS A VISIT

It was not long before life at the Harrington homestead settled into something like order — though not exactly the order that Miss Polly had at first prescribed. Pollyanna sewed, practised, read aloud, and studied cooking in the kitchen, it is true; but she did not give to any of these things quite so much time as had first been planned. She had more time, also, to " just live," as she expressed it, for almost all of every afternoon from two until six o'clock was hers to do with as she liked — provided she did not " like " to do certain things already prohibited by Aunt Polly.

It is a question, perhaps, whether all this leisure time was given to the child as a relief to Pollyanna from work — or as a relief to Aunt Polly from Pollyanna. Certainly, as those first July days passed, Miss Polly found occasion many times to ejaculate " What an extraordinary child! " and certainly the reading and sewing lessons found her at their conclusion each day somewhat dazed and wholly exhausted.

Nancy, in the kitchen, fared better. She was not dazed nor exhausted. Wednesdays and Saturdays came to be, indeed, red-letter days to her.

There were no children in the immediate neighborhood of the Harrington homestead for Pollyanna to play with. The house itself was on the outskirts of the village, and though there were other houses not far away, they did not chance to contain any boys or girls near Pollyanna's age. This, however, did not seem to disturb Pollyanna in the least.

"Oh, no, I don't mind it at all," she explained to Nancy. "I'm happy just to walk around and see the streets and the houses and watch the people. I just love people. Don't you, Nancy?"

"Well, I can't say I do — all of 'em," retorted Nancy, tersely.

Almost every pleasant afternoon found Pollyanna begging for "an errand to run," so that she might be off for a walk in one direction or another; and it was on these walks that frequently she met the Man. To herself Pollyanna always called him "the Man," no matter if she met a dozen other men the same day.

The Man often wore a long black coat and a high

silk hat — two things that the " just men " never wore. His face was clean shaven and rather pale, and his hair, showing below his hat, was somewhat gray. He walked erect, and rather rapidly, and he was always alone, which made Pollyanna vaguely sorry for him. Perhaps it was because of this that she one day spoke to him.

" How do you do, sir? Isn't this a nice day? " she called cheerily, as she approached him.

The man threw a hurried glance about him, then stopped uncertainly.

" Did you speak — to me? " he asked in a sharp voice.

" Yes, sir," beamed Pollyanna. " I say, it's a nice day, isn't it? "

" Eh? Oh! Humph! " he grunted; and strode on again.

Pollyanna laughed. He was such a funny man, she thought.

The next day she saw him again.

" 'Tisn't quite so nice as yesterday, but it's pretty nice," she called out cheerfully.

" Eh? Oh! Humph! " grunted the man as before; and once again Pollyanna laughed happily.

When for the third time Pollyanna accosted him in much the same manner, the man stopped abruptly.

" See here, child, who are you, and why are you speaking to me every day? "

" I'm Pollyanna Whittier, and I thought you looked lonesome. I'm so glad you stopped. Now we're introduced — only I don't know your name yet."

" Well, of all the — " The man did not finish his sentence, but strode on faster than ever.

Pollyanna looked after him with a disappointed droop to her usually smiling lips.

" Maybe he didn't understand — but that was only half an introduction. I don't know *his* name, yet," she murmured, as she proceeded on her way.

Pollyanna was carrying calf's-foot jelly to Mrs. Snow to-day. Miss Polly Harrington always sent something to Mrs. Snow once a week. She said she thought that it was her duty, inasmuch as Mrs. Snow was poor, sick, and a member of her church — it was the duty of all the church members to look out for her, of course. Miss Polly did her duty by Mrs. Snow usually on Thursday afternoons — not personally, but through Nancy. To-day Pollyanna had begged the privilege, and Nancy had promptly given it to her in accordance with Miss Polly's orders.

" And it's glad that I am ter get rid of it," Nancy

had declared in private afterwards to Pollyanna; "though it's a shame ter be tuckin' the job off on ter you, poor lamb, so it is, it is!"

"But I'd love to do it, Nancy."

"Well, you won't — after you've done it once," predicted Nancy, sourly.

"Why not?"

"Because nobody does. If folks wa'n't sorry for her there wouldn't a soul go near her from mornin' till night, she's that cantankerous. All is, I pity her daughter what *has* ter take care of her."

"But, why, Nancy?"

Nancy shrugged her shoulders.

"Well, in plain words, it's just that nothin' what ever *has* happened, has happened right in Mis' Snow's eyes. Even the days of the week ain't run ter her mind. If it's Monday she's bound ter say she wished 'twas Sunday; and if you take her jelly you're pretty sure ter hear she wanted chicken — but if you *did* bring her chicken, she'd be jest hankerin' for lamb broth!"

"Why, what a funny woman," laughed Pollyanna. "I think I shall like to go to see her. She must be so surprising and — and different. I love *different* folks."

"Humph! Well, Mis' Snow's 'different,' all

right — I hope, for the sake of the rest of us!"
Nancy had finished grimly.

Pollyanna was thinking of these remarks to-day
as she turned in at the gate of the shabby little cot-
tage. Her eyes were quite sparkling, indeed, at the
prospect of meeting this " different " Mrs. Snow.

A pale-faced, tired-looking young girl answered
her knock at the door.

" How do you do? " began Pollyanna politely.
" I'm from Miss Polly Harrington, and I'd like to
see Mrs. Snow, please."

" Well, if you would, you're the first one that
ever ' liked ' to see her," muttered the girl under
her breath; but Pollyanna did not hear this. The
girl had turned and was leading the way through
the hall to a door at the end of it.

In the sick-room, after the girl had ushered her
in and closed the door, Pollyanna blinked a little
before she could accustom her eyes to the gloom.
Then she saw, dimly outlined, a woman half-sitting
up in the bed across the room. Pollyanna advanced
at once.

" How do you do, Mrs. Snow? Aunt Polly says
she hopes you are comfortable to-day, and she's
sent you some calf's-foot jelly."

" Dear me! Jelly? " murmured a fretful voice.

"Of course I'm very much obliged, but I was hoping 'twould be lamb broth to-day."

Pollyanna frowned a little.

"Why, I thought it was *chicken* you wanted when folks brought you jelly," she said.

"What?" The sick woman turned sharply.

"Why, nothing, much," apologized Pollyanna, hurriedly; "and of course it doesn't really make any difference. It's only that Nancy said it was chicken you wanted when we brought jelly, and lamb broth when we brought chicken — but maybe 'twas the other way, and Nancy forgot."

The sick woman pulled herself up till she sat erect in the bed — a most unusual thing for her to do, though Pollyanna did not know this.

"Well, Miss Impertinence, who are you?" she demanded.

Pollyanna laughed gleefully.

"Oh, *that* isn't my name, Mrs. Snow — and I'm so glad 'tisn't, too! That would be worse than 'Hephzibah,' wouldn't it? I'm Pollyanna Whittier, Miss Polly Harrington's niece, and I've come to live with her. That's why I'm here with the jelly this morning."

All through the first part of this sentence, the sick woman had sat interestedly erect; but at the reference to the jelly she fell back on her pillow listlessly.

"Very well; thank you. Your aunt is very kind, of course, but my appetite isn't very good this morning, and I was wanting lamb —" She stopped suddenly, then went on with an abrupt change of subject. "I never slept a wink last night — not a wink!"

"O dear, I wish *I* didn't," sighed Pollyanna, placing the jelly on the little stand and seating herself comfortably in the nearest chair. "You lose such a lot of time just sleeping! Don't you think so?"

"Lose time — sleeping!" exclaimed the sick woman.

"Yes, when you might be just living, you know. It seems such a pity we can't live nights, too."

Once again the woman pulled herself erect in her bed.

"Well, if you ain't the amazing young one!" she cried. "Here! do you go to that window and pull up the curtain," she directed. "I should like to know what you look like!"

Pollyanna rose to her feet, but she laughed a little ruefully.

"O dear! then you'll see my freckles, won't

you?" she sighed, as she went to the window; " — and just when I was being so glad it was dark and you couldn't see 'em. There! Now you can — oh!" she broke off excitedly, as she turned back to the bed; "I'm so glad you wanted to see me, because now I can see you! They didn't tell me you were so pretty!"

"Me! — pretty!" scoffed the woman, bitterly.

"Why, yes. Didn't you know it?" cried Pollyanna.

"Well, no, I didn't," retorted Mrs. Snow, dryly. Mrs. Snow had lived forty years, and for fifteen of those years she had been too busy wishing things were different to find much time to enjoy things as they were.

"Oh, but your eyes are so big and dark, and your hair's all dark, too, and curly," cooed Pollyanna. "I love black curls. (That's one of the things I'm going to have when I get to Heaven.) And you've got two little red spots in your cheeks. Why, Mrs. Snow, you *are* pretty! I should think you'd know it when you looked at yourself in the glass."

"The glass!" snapped the sick woman, falling back on her pillow. "Yes, well, I hain't done much prinkin' before the mirror these days — and you wouldn't, if you was flat on your back as I am!"

"Why, no, of course not," agreed Pollyanna, sympathetically. "But wait — just let me show you," she exclaimed, skipping over to the bureau and picking up a small hand-glass.

On the way back to the bed she stopped, eyeing the sick woman with a critical gaze.

"I reckon maybe, if you don't mind, I'd like to fix your hair just a little before I let you see it," she proposed. "May I fix your hair, please?"

"Why, I — suppose so, if you want to," permitted Mrs. Snow, grudgingly; "but 'twon't stay, you know."

"Oh, thank you. I love to fix people's hair," exulted Pollyanna, carefully laying down the hand-glass and reaching for a comb. "I sha'n't do much to-day, of course — I'm in such a hurry for you to see how pretty you are; but some day I'm going to take it all down and have a perfectly lovely time with it," she cried, touching with soft fingers the waving hair above the sick woman's forehead.

For five minutes Pollyanna worked swiftly, deftly, combing a refractory curl into fluffiness, perking up a drooping ruffle at the neck, or shaking a pillow into plumpness so that the head might have a better pose. Meanwhile the sick woman, frowning prodigiously, and openly scoffing at the whole procedure, was, in spite of herself, beginning to tingle with a feeling perilously near to excitement.

"There!" panted Pollyanna, hastily plucking a pink from a vase near by and tucking it into the dark hair where it would give the best effect. "Now I reckon we're ready to be looked at!" And she held out the mirror in triumph.

"Humph!" grunted the sick woman, eyeing her reflection severely. "I like red pinks better than pink ones; but then, it'll fade, anyhow, before night, so what's the difference!"

"But I should think you'd be glad they did fade," laughed Pollyanna, "'cause then you can have the fun of getting some more. I just love your hair fluffed out like that," she finished with a satisfied gaze. "Don't you?"

"Hm-m; maybe. Still — 'twon't last, with me tossing back and forth on the pillow as I do."

"Of course not — and I'm glad, too," nodded Pollyanna, cheerfully, "because then I can fix it again. Anyhow, I should think *you'd* be glad it's black — black shows up so much nicer on a pillow than yellow hair like mine does."

"Maybe; but I never did set much store by black hair — shows gray too soon," retorted Mrs. Snow.

She spoke fretfully, but she still held the mirror before her face.

"Oh, I love black hair! I should be so glad if I only had it," sighed Pollyanna.

Mrs. Snow dropped the mirror and turned irritably.

"Well, you wouldn't! — not if you were me. You wouldn't be glad for black hair nor anything else — if you had to lie here all day as I do!"

Pollyanna bent her brows in a thoughtful frown.

"Why, 'twould be kind of hard — to do it then, wouldn't it?" she mused aloud.

"Do what?"

"Be glad about things."

"Be glad about things — when you're sick in bed all your days? Well, I should say it would," retorted Mrs. Snow. "If you don't think so, just tell me something to be glad about; that's all!"

To Mrs. Snow's unbounded amazement, Pollyanna sprang to her feet and clapped her hands.

"Oh, goody! That'll be a hard one — won't it? I've got to go, now, but I'll think and think all the way home; and maybe the next time I come I can tell it to you. Good-by. I've had a lovely time! Good-by," she called again, as she tripped through the doorway.

"Well, I never! Now, what does she mean by that?" ejaculated Mrs. Snow, staring after her visitor. By and by she turned her head and picked up the mirror, eyeing her reflection critically.

"That little thing *has* got a knack with hair — and no mistake," she muttered under her breath. "I declare, I didn't know it could look so pretty. But then, what's the use?" she sighed, dropping the little glass into the bedclothes, and rolling her head on the pillow fretfully.

A little later, when Milly, Mrs. Snow's daughter, came in, the mirror still lay among the bedclothes — though it had been carefully hidden from sight.

"Why, mother — the curtain is up!" cried Milly, dividing her amazed stare between the window and the pink in her mother's hair.

"Well, what if it is?" snapped the sick woman. 'I needn't stay in the dark all my life, if I am sick, need I?"

"Why, n-no, of course not," rejoined Milly, in hasty conciliation, as she reached for the medicine bottle. "It's only — well, you know very well that I've tried to get you to have a lighter room for ages — and you wouldn't."

There was no reply to this. Mrs. Snow was pick-

ing at the lace on her nightgown.   At last she spoke
fretfully.

" I should think *somebody* might give me a new
nightdress — instead of lamb broth, for a change ! "

" Why — mother ! "

No wonder Milly quite gasped aloud with bewil-
derment.   In the drawer behind her at that moment
lay two new nightdresses that Milly for months had
been vainly urging her mother to wear.

CHAPTER IX

WHICH TELLS OF THE MAN

It rained the next time Pollyanna saw the Man. She greeted him, however, with a bright smile.

" It isn't so nice to-day, is it? " she called blithesomely. " I'm glad it doesn't rain always, anyhow! "

The man did not even grunt this time, nor turn his head. Pollyanna decided that of course he did not hear her. The next time, therefore (which happened to be the following day), she spoke up louder. She thought it particularly necessary to do this, anyway, for the Man was striding along, his hands behind his back, and his eyes on the ground — which seemed, to Pollyanna, preposterous in the face of the glorious sunshine and the freshly-washed morning air: Pollyanna, as a special treat, was on a morning errand to-day.

" How do you do? " she chirped. " I'm so glad it isn't yesterday, aren't you? "

The man stopped abruptly. There was an angry scowl on his face.

"See here, little girl, we might just as well settle this thing right now, once for all," he began testily. "I've got something besides the weather to think of. I don't know whether the sun shines or not."

Pollyanna beamed joyously.

"No, sir; I thought you didn't. That's why I told you."

"Yes; well — Eh? What?" he broke off sharply, in sudden understanding of her words.

"I say, that's why I told you — so you would notice it, you know — that the sun shines, and all that. I knew you'd be glad it did if you only stopped to think of it — and you didn't look a bit as if you *were* thinking of it!"

"Well, of all the — " ejaculated the man, with an oddly impotent gesture. He started forward again, but after the second step he turned back, still frowning.

"See here, why don't you find some one your own age to talk to?"

"I'd like to, sir, but there aren't any 'round here, Nancy says. Still, I don't mind so very much. I like old folks just as well, maybe better, sometimes — being used to the Ladies' Aid, so."

" Humph! The Ladies' Aid, indeed! Is that what you took me for? " The man's lips were threatening to smile, but the scowl above them was still trying to hold them grimly stern.

Pollyanna laughed gleefully.

" Oh, no, sir. You don't look a mite like a Ladies' Aider — not but that you're just as good, of course — maybe better," she added in hurried politeness. " You see, I'm sure you're much nicer than you look! "

The man made a queer noise in his throat.

" Well, of all the — " he ejaculated again, as he turned and strode on as before.

The next time Pollyanna met the Man, his eyes were gazing straight into hers, with a quizzical directness that made his face look really pleasant, Pollyanna thought.

" Good afternoon," he greeted her a little stiffly. " Perhaps I'd better say right away that I *know* the sun is shining to-day."

" But you don't have to tell me," nodded Pollyanna, brightly. " I *knew* you knew it just as soon as I saw you."

" Oh, you did, did you? "

" Yes, sir; I saw it in your eyes, you know, and in your smile."

" Humph!" grunted the man, as he passed on.

The Man always spoke to Pollyanna after this, and frequently he spoke first, though usually he said little but " good afternoon." Even that, however, was a great surprise to Nancy, who chanced to be with Pollyanna one day when the greeting was given.

" Sakes alive, Miss Pollyanna," she gasped, " did that man *speak* to *you?*"

" Why, yes, he always does — now," smiled Pollyanna.

"' He always does'! Goodness! Do you know who — he — is?" demanded Nancy.

Pollyanna frowned and shook her head.

" I reckon he forgot to tell me one day. You see, I did my part of the introducing, but he didn't."

Nancy's eyes widened.

" But he never speaks ter anybody, child — he hain't for years, I guess, except when he just has to, for business, and all that. He's John Pendleton. He lives all by himself in the big house on Pendleton Hill. He won't even have any one 'round ter cook for him — comes down ter the hotel for his meals three times a day. I know Sally Miner, who waits on him, and she says he hardly opens his head

enough ter tell what he wants ter eat. She has ter
guess it more'n half the time — only it'll be somethin' *cheap!* She knows that without no tellin'.'"

Pollyanna nodded sympathetically.

"I know. You have to look for cheap things
when you're poor. Father and I took meals out a
lot. We had beans and fish balls most generally.
We used to say how glad we were we liked beans
— that is, we said it specially when we were looking
at the roast turkey place, you know, that was sixty
cents. Does Mr. Pendleton like beans?"

"Like 'em! What if he does — or don't? Why,
Miss Pollyanna, he ain't poor. He's got loads of
money, John Pendleton has — from his father.
There ain't nobody in town as rich as he is. He
could eat dollar bills, if he wanted to — and not
know it."

Pollyanna giggled.

"As if anybody *could* eat dollar bills and not
know it, Nancy, when they come to try to chew
'em!"

"Ho! I mean he's rich enough ter do it,"
shrugged Nancy. "He ain't spendin' his money,
that's all. He's a-savin' of it."

"Oh, for the heathen," surmised Pollyanna.
"How perfectly splendid! That's denying your-

self and taking up your cross. I know; father told
me."

Nancy's lips parted abruptly, as if there were
angry words all ready to come; but her eyes, resting on Pollyanna's jubilantly trustful face, saw
something that prevented the words being spoken.

" Humph! " she vouchsafed. Then, showing her
old-time interest, she went on: " But, say, it *is*
queer, his speakin' to you, honestly, Miss Pollyanna.
He don't speak ter no one; and he lives all alone
in a great big lovely house all full of jest grand
things, they say. Some says he's crazy, and some
jest cross; and some says he's got a skeleton in his
closet."

" Oh, Nancy! " shuddered Pollyanna. " How
can he keep such a dreadful thing? I should think
he'd throw it away! "

Nancy chuckled. That Pollyanna had taken the
skeleton literally instead of figuratively, she knew
very well; but, perversely, she refrained from cor-
recting the mistake.

" And *everybody* says he's mysterious," she went
on. " Some years he jest travels, week in and week
out, and it's always in heathen countries — Egypt
and Asia and the Desert of Sarah, you know."

" Oh, a missionary," nodded Pollyanna.

Nancy laughed oddly.

" Well, I didn't say that, Miss Pollyanna. When he comes back he writes books — queer, odd books, they say, about some gimcrack he's found in them heathen countries. But he don't never seem ter want ter spend no money here — leastways, not for jest livin'."

" Of course not — if he's saving it for the heathen," declared Pollyanna. " But he is a funny man, and he's different, too, just like Mrs. Snow, only he's a different different."

" Well, I guess he is — rather," chuckled Nancy.

" I'm gladder'n ever now, anyhow, that he speaks to me," sighed Pollyanna contentedly.

CHAPTER X

A SURPRISE FOR MRS. SNOW

THE next time Pollyanna went to see Mrs. Snow, she found that lady, as at first, in a darkened room.

"It's the little girl from Miss Polly's, mother," announced Milly, in a tired manner; then Pollyanna found herself alone with the invalid.

"Oh, it's you, is it?" asked a fretful voice from the bed. "I remember you. *Any*body'd remember you, I guess, if they saw you once. I wish you had come yesterday. I *wanted* you yesterday."

"Did you? Well, I'm glad 'tisn't any farther away from yesterday than to-day is, then," laughed Pollyanna, advancing cheerily into the room, and setting her basket carefully down on a chair. "My! but aren't you dark here, though? I can't see you a bit," she cried, unhesitatingly crossing to the window and pulling up the shade. "I want to see if you've fixed your hair like I did —oh, you haven't! But, never mind; I'm glad you haven't, after all.

'cause maybe you'll let me do it — later. But *now* I want you to see what I've brought you."

The woman stirred restlessly.

" Just as if how it looks would make any difference in how it tastes," she scoffed — but she turned her eyes toward the basket. " Well, what is it? "

" Guess! What do you want? " Pollyanna had skipped back to the basket. Her face was alight.

The sick woman frowned.

" Why, I don't *want* anything, as I know of," she sighed. " After all, they all taste alike! "

Pollyanna chuckled.

" This won't. Guess! If you *did* want something, what would it be? "

The woman hesitated. She did not realize it herself, but she had so long been accustomed to wanting what she did not have, that to state off-hand what she *did* want seemed impossible — until she knew what she had. Obviously, however, she must say something. This extraordinary child was waiting.

" Well, of course, there's lamb broth — "

" I've got it! " crowed Pollyanna.

" But that's what I *didn't* want," sighed the sick woman, sure now of what her stomach craved. " It was chicken I wanted."

"Oh, I've got that, too," chuckled Pollyanna.

The woman turned in amazement.

"Both of them?" she demanded.

"Yes — and calf's-foot jelly," triumphed Polly-anna. "I was just bound you should have what you wanted for once; so Nancy and I fixed it. Oh, of course, there's only a little of each — but there's *some* of all of 'em! I'm so glad you did want chicken," she went on contentedly, as she lifted the three little bowls from her basket. "You see, I got to thinking on the way here — what if you should say tripe, or onions, or something like that, that I didn't have! Wouldn't it have been a shame — when I'd tried so hard?" she laughed merrily.

There was no reply. The sick woman seemed to be trying — mentally — to find something she had lost.

"There! I'm to leave them all," announced Polly-anna, as she arranged the three bowls in a row on the table. "Like enough it'll be lamb broth you want to-morrow. How do you do to-day?" she finished in polite inquiry.

"Very poorly, thank you," murmured Mrs. Snow, falling back into her usual listless attitude. "I lost my nap this morning. Nellie Higgins next door has begun music lessons, and her practising drives me nearly wild. She was at it all the morning — every minute! I'm sure, I don't know what I shall do!"

Polly nodded sympathetically.

"I know. It *is* awful! Mrs. White had it once — one of my Ladies' Aiders, you know. She had rheumatic fever, too, at the same time, so she couldn't thrash 'round. She said 'twould have been easier if she could have. Can you?"

"Can I — what?"

"Thrash 'round — move, you know, so as to change your position when the music gets too hard to stand."

Mrs. Snow stared a little.

"Why, of course I can move — anywhere — in bed," she rejoined a little irritably.

"Well, you can be glad of that, then, anyhow, can't you?" nodded Pollyanna. "Mrs. White couldn't. You can't thrash when you have rheumatic fever — though you want to something awful, Mrs. White says. She told me afterwards she reckoned she'd have gone raving crazy if it hadn't been for Mr. White's sister's ears — being deaf, so."

"Sister's — *ears!* What do you mean?"

Pollyanna laughed.

"Well, I reckon I didn't tell it all, and I forgot

you didn't know Mrs. White. You see, Miss White
was deaf — awfully deaf; and she came to visit
'em and to help take care of Mrs. White and the
house. Well, they had such an awful time making
her understand *anything,* that after that, every time
the piano commenced to play across the street, Mrs.
White felt so glad she *could* hear it, that she didn't
mind so much that she *did* hear it, 'cause she
couldn't help thinking how awful 'twould be if she
was deaf and couldn't hear anything, like her husband's sister. You see, she was playing the game,
too. I'd told her about it."

"The — game?"

Pollyanna clapped her hands.

"There! I 'most forgot; but I've thought it up,
Mrs. Snow — what you can be glad about."

"*Glad* about! What do you mean?"

"Why, I told you I would. Don't you remember? You asked me to tell you something to be
glad about — glad, you know, even though you did
have to lie here abed all day."

"Oh!" scoffed the woman. "*That?* Yes, I
remember that; but I didn't suppose you were in
earnest any more than I was."

"Oh, yes, I was," nodded Pollyanna, triumphantly; "and I found it, too. But 'twas hard.

It's all the more fun, though, always, when 'tis hard.
And I will own up, honest to true, that I couldn't
think of anything for a while. Then I got it."

"Did you, really? Well, what is it?" Mrs.
Snow's voice was sarcastically polite.

Pollyanna drew a long breath.

"I thought — how glad you could be — that
other folks weren't like you — all sick in bed like
this, you know," she announced impressively.

Mrs. Snow stared. Her eyes were angry.

"Well, really!" she ejaculated then, in not quite
an agreeable tone of voice.

"And now I'll tell you the game," proposed
Pollyanna, blithely confident. "It'll be just lovely
for you to play — it'll be so hard. And there's so
much more fun when it is hard! You see, it's like
this." And she began to tell of the missionary barrel, the crutches, and the doll that did not come.

The story was just finished when Milly appeared
at the door.

"Your aunt is wanting you, Miss Pollyanna,"
she said with dreary listlessness. "She telephoned
down to the Harlows' across the way. She says
you're to hurry — that you've got some practising
to make up before dark."

Pollyanna rose reluctantly.

"All right," she sighed. "I'll hurry." Suddenly she laughed. "I suppose I ought to be glad I've got legs to hurry with, hadn't I, Mrs. Snow?"

There was no answer. Mrs. Snow's eyes were closed. But Milly, whose eyes were wide open with surprise, saw that there were tears on the wasted cheeks.

"Good-by," flung Pollyanna over her shoulder, as she reached the door. "I'm awfully sorry about the hair — I wanted to do it. But maybe I can next time!"

One by one the July days passed. To Pollyanna, they were happy days, indeed. She often told her aunt, joyously, how very happy they were. Whereupon her aunt would usually reply, wearily:

"Very well, Pollyanna. I am gratified, of course, that they are happy; but I trust that they are profitable, as well — otherwise I should have failed signally in my duty."

Generally Pollyanna would answer this with a hug and a kiss — a proceeding that was still always most disconcerting to Miss Polly; but one day she spoke. It was during the sewing hour.

"Do you mean that it wouldn't be enough then,

Aunt Polly, that they should be just happy days?'"
she asked wistfully.

"That is what I mean, Pollyanna."

"They must be pro-fi-ta-ble as well?"

"Certainly."

"What is being pro-fi-ta-ble?"

"Why, it — it's just being profitable — having
profit, something to show for it, Pollyanna. What
an extraordinary child you are!"

"Then just being glad isn't pro-fi-ta-ble?" questioned Pollyanna, a little anxiously.

"Certainly not."

"O dear! Then you wouldn't like it, of course.
I'm afraid, now, you won't ever play the game,
Aunt Polly."

"Game? What game?"

"Why, that father —" Pollyanna clapped her
hand to her lips. "N-nothing," she stammered.

Miss Polly frowned.

"That will do for this morning, Pollyanna," she
said tersely. And the sewing lesson was over.

It was that afternoon that Pollyanna, coming
down from her attic room, met her aunt on the
stairway.

"Why, Aunt Polly, how perfectly lovely!" she
cried. "You were coming up to see me! Come

right in. I love company," she finished, scampering
up the stairs and throwing her door wide open.

Now Miss Polly had not been intending to call
on her niece. She had been planning to look for
a certain white wool shawl in the cedar chest near
the east window. But to her unbounded surprise
now, she found herself, not in the main attic before
the cedar chest, but in Pollyanna's little room sitting
in one of the straight-backed chairs — so many,
many times since Pollyanna came, Miss Polly had
found herself like this, doing some utterly unex-
pected, surprising thing, quite unlike the thing she
had set out to do!

"I love company," said Pollyanna, again, flitting
about as if she were dispensing the hospitality of a
palace; "specially since I've had this room, all
mine, you know. Oh, of course, I had a room,
always, but 'twas a hired room, and hired rooms
aren't half as nice as owned ones, are they? And
of course I do own this one, don't I?"

"Why, y-yes, Pollyanna," murmured Miss Polly,
vaguely wondering why she did not get up at once
and go to look for that shawl.

"And of course now I just love this room, even
if it hasn't got the carpets and curtains and pictures
that I'd been want—" With a painful blush Polly-

anna stopped short. She was plunging into an entirely different sentence when her aunt interrupted her sharply.

" What's that, Pollyanna? "

" N-nothing, Aunt Polly, truly. I didn't mean to say it."

" Probably not," returned Miss Polly, coldly; " but you did say it, so suppose we have the rest of it."

" But it wasn't anything only that I'd been kind of planning on pretty carpets and lace curtains and things, you know. But, of course — "

" *Planning* on them! " interrupted Miss Polly, sharply.

Pollyanna blushed still more painfully.

" I ought not to have, of course, Aunt Polly," she apologized. " It was only because I'd always wanted them and hadn't had them, I suppose. Oh, we'd had two rugs in the barrels, but they were little, you know, and one had ink spots, and the other holes; and there never were only those two pictures; the one fath— I mean the good one we sold, and the bad one that broke. Of course if it hadn't been for all that I shouldn't have wanted them, so — pretty things, I mean; and I shouldn't have got to planning all through the hall that first

day how pretty mine would be here, and — and —
But, truly, Aunt Polly, it wasn't but just a minute
— I mean, a few minutes — before I was being
glad that the bureau *didn't* have a looking-glass,
because it didn't show my freckles; and there
couldn't be a nicer picture than the one out my
window there; and you've been so good to me,
that — "

Miss Polly rose suddenly to her feet. Her face
was very red.

"That will do, Pollyanna," she said stiffly.
"You have said quite enough, I'm sure." The next
minute she had swept down the stairs — and not
until she reached the first floor did it suddenly occur
to her that she had gone up into the attic to find a
white wool shawl in the cedar chest near the east
window.

Less than twenty-four hours later, Miss Polly
said to Nancy, crisply:

"Nancy, you may move Miss Pollyanna's things
down-stairs this morning to the room directly beneath. I have decided to have my niece sleep there
for the present."

"Yes, ma'am," said Nancy aloud.

"O glory!" said Nancy to herself.

To Pollyanna, a minute later, she cried joyously:

"And won't ye jest be listenin' ter this, Miss Pollyanna. You're ter sleep down-stairs in the room straight under this. You are — you are!"

Pollyanna actually grew white.

"You mean — why, Nancy, not really — really and truly?"

"I guess you'll think it's really and truly," prophesied Nancy, exultingly, nodding her head to Pollyanna over the armful of dresses she had taken from the closet. "I'm told ter take down yer things, and I'm goin' ter take 'em, too, 'fore she gets a chance ter change her mind."

Pollyanna did not stop to hear the end of this sentence. At the imminent risk of being dashed headlong, she was flying down-stairs, two steps at a time.

Bang went two doors and a chair before Pollyanna at last reached her goal — Aunt Polly.

"Oh, Aunt Polly, Aunt Polly, did you mean it, really? Why, that room's got *everything* — the carpet and curtains and three pictures, besides the one outdoors, too, 'cause the windows look the same way. Oh, Aunt Polly!"

"Very well, Pollyanna. I am gratified that you like the change, of course; but if you think so much of all those things, I trust you will take proper care of them; that's all. Pollyanna, please pick up that chair; and you have banged two doors in the last half-minute." Miss Polly spoke sternly, all the more sternly because, for some inexplicable reason, she felt inclined to cry — and Miss Polly was not used to feeling inclined to cry.

Pollyanna picked up the chair.

"Yes'm; I know I banged 'em — those doors," she admitted cheerfully. "You see I'd just found out about the room, and I reckon you'd have banged doors if — " Pollyanna stopped short and eyed her aunt with new interest. "Aunt Polly, *did* you ever bang doors?"

"I hope — not, Pollyanna!" Miss Polly's voice was properly shocked.

"Why, Aunt Polly, what a shame!" Pollyanna's face expressed only concerned sympathy.

"A shame!" repeated Aunt Polly, too dazed to say more.

"Why, yes. You see, if you'd felt like banging doors you'd have banged 'em, of course; and if you didn't, that must have meant that you weren't ever glad over anything — or you would have banged 'em. You couldn't have helped it. And I'm so sorry you weren't ever glad over anything!"

"Pollyanna!" gasped the lady; but Pollyanna

was gone, and only the distant bang of the attic-stairway door answered for her. Pollyanna had gone to help Nancy bring down " her things."

Miss Polly, in the sitting room, felt vaguely disturbed; — but then, of course she *had* been glad — over some things!

CHAPTER XI

AUGUST came. August brought several surprises and some changes — none of which, however, were really a surprise to Nancy. Nancy, since Pollyanna's arrival, had come to look for surprises and changes.

First there was the kitten.

Pollyanna found the kitten mewing pitifully some distance down the road. When systematic questioning of the neighbors failed to find any one who claimed it, Pollyanna brought it home at once, as a matter of course.

"And I was glad I didn't find any one who owned it, too," she told her aunt in happy confidence; "'cause I wanted to bring it home all the time. I love kitties. I knew you'd be glad to let it live here."

Miss Polly looked at the forlorn little gray bunch of neglected misery in Pollyanna's arms, and shivered: Miss Polly did not care for cats — not even pretty, healthy, clean ones.

"Ugh! Pollyanna! What a dirty little beast! And it's sick, I'm sure, and all mangy and fleay."

"I know it, poor little thing," crooned Pollyanna, tenderly, looking into the little creature's frightened eyes. "And it's all trembly, too, it's so scared. You see it doesn't know, yet, that we're going to keep it, of course."

"No — nor anybody else," retorted Miss Polly, with meaning emphasis.

"Oh, yes, they do," nodded Pollyanna, entirely misunderstanding her aunt's words. "I told everybody we should keep it, if I didn't find where it belonged. I knew you'd be glad to have it — poor little lonesome thing!"

Miss Polly opened her lips and tried to speak; but in vain. The curious helpless feeling that had been hers so often since Pollyanna's arrival, had her now fast in its grip.

"Of course I knew," hurried on Pollyanna, gratefully, "that you wouldn't let a dear little lonesome kitty go hunting for a home when you'd just taken *me* in; and I said so to Mrs. Ford when she asked if you'd let me keep it. Why, *I* had the Ladies' Aid, you know, and kitty didn't have anybody. I knew you'd feel that way," she nodded happily, as she ran from the room.

" But, Pollyanna, Pollyanna," remonstrated Miss Polly. " I don't — " But Pollyanna was already halfway to the kitchen, calling:

" Nancy, Nancy, just see this dear little kitty that Aunt Polly is going to bring up along with me!" And Aunt Polly, in the sitting room — who abhorred cats — fell back in her chair with a gasp of dismay, powerless to remonstrate.

The next day it was a dog, even dirtier and more forlorn, perhaps, than was the kitten; and again Miss Polly, to her dumfounded amazement, found herself figuring as a kind protector and an angel of mercy — a rôle that Pollyanna so unhesitatingly thrust upon her as a matter of course, that the woman — who abhorred dogs even more than she did cats, if possible — found herself as before, powerless to remonstrate.

When, in less than a week, however, Pollyanna brought home a small, ragged boy, and confidently claimed the same protection for him, Miss Polly did have something to say. It happened after this wise.

On a pleasant Thursday morning Pollyanna had been taking calf's-foot jelly again to Mrs. Snow.

Mrs. Snow and Pollyanna were the best of friends now. Their friendship had started from the third visit Pollyanna had made, the one after she had told Mrs. Snow of the game. Mrs. Snow herself was playing the game now, with Pollyanna. To be sure, she was not playing it very well — she had been sorry for everything for so long, that it was not easy to be glad for anything now. But under Pollyanna's cheery instructions and merry laughter at her mistakes, she was learning fast. To-day, even, to Pollyanna's huge delight, she had said that she was glad Pollyanna brought calf's-foot jelly, because that was just what she had been wanting — she did not know that Milly, at the front door, had told Pollyanna that the minister's wife had already that day sent over a great bowlful of that same kind of jelly.

Pollyanna was thinking of this now when suddenly she saw the boy.

The boy was sitting in a disconsolate little heap by the roadside, whittling half-heartedly at a small stick.

"Hullo," smiled Pollyanna, engagingly.

The boy glanced up, but he looked away again, at once.

"Hullo yourself," he mumbled.

Pollyanna laughed.

" Now you don't look as if you'd be glad even for calf's-foot jelly," she chuckled, stopping before him.

The boy stirred restlessly, gave her a surprised look, and began to whittle again at his stick, with the dull, broken-bladed knife in his hand.

Pollyanna hesitated, then dropped herself comfortably down on the grass near him. In spite of Pollyanna's brave assertion that she was " used to Ladies' Aiders," and " didn't mind," she had sighed at times for some companion of her own age. Hence her determination to make the most of this one.

" My name's Pollyanna Whittier," she began pleasantly. " What's yours? "

Again the boy stirred restlessly. He even almost got to his feet. But he settled back.

" Jimmy Bean," he grunted with ungracious indifference.

" Good! Now we're introduced. I'm glad you did your part — some folks don't, you know. I live at Miss Polly Harrington's house. Where do you live? "

" Nowhere."

"Nowhere! Why, you can't do that — everybody lives somewhere," asserted Pollyanna.

"Well, I don't — just now. I'm huntin' up a new place."

"Oh! Where is it?"

The boy regarded her with scornful eyes.

"Silly! As if I'd be a-huntin' for it — if I knew!"

Pollyanna tossed her head a little. This was not a nice boy, and she did not like to be called "silly." Still, he was somebody besides — old folks.

"Where did you live — before?" she queried.

"Well, if you ain't the beat'em for askin' questions!" sighed the boy impatiently.

"I have to be," retorted Pollyanna calmly, "else I couldn't find out a thing about you. If you'd talk more I wouldn't talk so much."

The boy gave a short laugh. It was a sheepish laugh, and not quite a willing one; but his face looked a little pleasanter when he spoke this time.

"All right then — here goes! I'm Jimmy Bean, and I'm ten years old goin' on eleven. I come last year ter live at the Orphans' Home; but they've got so many kids there ain't much room for me, an' I wa'n't never wanted, anyhow, I don't

believe. So I've quit. I'm goin' ter live somewheres else — but I hain't found the place, yet. I'd
like a home — jest a common one, ye know, with
a mother in it, instead of a Matron. If ye has a
home, ye has folks; an' I hain't had folks since —
dad died. So I'm a-huntin' now. I've tried four
houses, but — they didn't want me — though I
said I expected ter work, 'course. There! Is that
all you want ter know?" The boy's voice had
broken a little over the last two sentences.

"Why, what a shame!" sympathized Pollyanna.
"And didn't there anybody want you? O dear! I
know just how you feel, because after — after my
father died, too, there wasn't anybody but the
Ladies' Aid for me, until Aunt Polly said she'd
take —" Pollyanna stopped abruptly. The dawn-
ing of a wonderful idea began to show in her
face.

"Oh, I know just the place for you," she cried.
"Aunt Polly'll take you — I know she will! Didn't
she take me? And didn't she take Fluffy and
Buffy, when they didn't have any one to love them,
or any place to go? — and they're only cats and
dogs. Oh, come, I know Aunt Polly'll take you!
You don't know how good and kind she is!"

Jimmy Bean's thin little face brightened.

"Honest Injun? Would she, now? I'd work, ye know, an' I'm real strong!" He bared a small, bony arm.

"Of course she would! Why, my Aunt Polly is the nicest lady in the world — now that my mama has gone to be a Heaven angel. And there's rooms — heaps of 'em," she continued, springing to her feet, and tugging at his arm. "It's an awful big house. Maybe, though," she added a little anxiously, as they hurried on, "maybe you'll have to sleep in the attic room. I did, at first. But there's screens there now, so 'twon't be so hot, and the flies can't get in, either, to bring in the germ-things on their feet. Did you know about that? It's perfectly lovely! Maybe she'll let you read the book if you're good — I mean, if you're bad. And you've got freckles, too," — with a critical glance — "so you'll be glad there isn't any looking-glass; and the outdoor picture is nicer than any wall-one could be, so you won't mind sleeping in that room at all, I'm sure," panted Pollyanna, finding suddenly that she needed the rest of her breath for purposes other than talking.

"Gorry!" exclaimed Jimmy Bean tersely and uncomprehendingly, but admiringly. Then he added: "I shouldn't think anybody who could talk like that, runnin', would need ter ask no questions ter fill up time with!"

Pollyanna laughed.

"Well, anyhow, you can be glad of that," she retorted; "for when I'm talking, *you* don't have to!"

When the house was reached, Pollyanna unhesitatingly piloted her companion straight into the presence of her amazed aunt.

"Oh, Aunt Polly," she triumphed. "Just look a-here! I've got something ever so much nicer, even, than Fluffy and Buffy for you to bring up. It's a real live boy. He won't mind a bit sleeping in the attic, at first, you know, and he says he'll work; but I shall need him the most of the time to play with, I reckon."

Miss Polly grew white, then very red. She did not quite understand; but she thought she understood enough.

"Pollyanna, what does this mean? Who is this dirty little boy? Where did you find him?" she demanded sharply.

The "dirty little boy" fell back a step and looked toward the door. Pollyanna laughed merrily.

" There, if I didn't forget to tell you his name!
I'm as bad as the Man. And he is dirty, too, isn't
he? — I mean, the boy is — just like Fluffy and
Buffy were when you took them in. But I reckon
he'll improve all right by washing, just as they did,
and — Oh, I 'most forgot again," she broke off
with a laugh. " This is Jimmy Bean, Aunt Polly."

" Well, what is he doing here? "

" Why, Aunt Polly, I just told you! " Pollyanna's eyes were wide with surprise. " He's for
you. I brought him home — so he could live here,
you know. He wants a home and folks. I told
him how good you were to me, and to Fluffy and
Buffy, and that I knew you would be to him, because of course he's even nicer than cats and dogs."

Miss Polly dropped back in her chair and raised
a shaking hand to her throat. The old helplessness
was threatening once more to overcome her. With
a visible struggle, however, Miss Polly pulled herself suddenly erect.

" That will do, Pollyanna. This is a little the
most absurd thing you've done yet. As if tramp
cats and mangy dogs weren't bad enough but you
must needs bring home ragged little beggars from
the street, who — "

There was a sudden stir from the boy. His eyes

flashed and his chin came up. With two strides of his sturdy little legs he confronted Miss Polly fearlessly.

"I ain't a beggar, marm, an' I don't want nothin' o' you. I was cal'latin' ter work, of course, fur my board an' keep. I wouldn't have come ter your old house, anyhow, if this 'ere girl hadn't 'a' made me, a-tellin' me how you was so good an' kind that you'd be jest dyin' ter take me in. So, there!" And he wheeled about and stalked from the room with a dignity that would have been absurd had it not been so pitiful.

"Oh, Aunt Polly," choked Pollyanna. "Why, I thought you'd be *glad* to have him here! I'm sure, I should think you'd be glad — "

Miss Polly raised her hand with a peremptory gesture of silence. Miss Polly's nerves had snapped at last. The "good and kind" of the boy's words were still ringing in her ears, and the old helplessness was almost upon her, she knew. Yet she rallied her forces with the last atom of her will power.

"Pollyanna," she cried sharply, "*will* you stop using that everlasting word 'glad'! It's 'glad' — 'glad' — 'glad' from morning till night until I think I shall grow wild!"

From sheer amazement Pollyanna's jaw dropped.

"Why, Aunt Polly," she breathed, "I should think you'd be glad to have me gl— Oh!" she broke off, clapping her hand to her lips and hurrying blindly from the room.

Before the boy had reached the end of the driveway, Pollyanna overtook him.

"Boy! Boy! Jimmy Bean, I want you to know how — how sorry I am," she panted, catching him with a detaining hand.

"Sorry nothin'! I ain't blamin' you," retorted the boy, sullenly. "But I ain't no beggar!" he added, with sudden spirit.

"Of course you aren't! But you mustn't blame auntie," appealed Pollyanna. "Probably I didn't do the introducing right, anyhow; and I reckon I didn't tell her much who you were. She *is* good and kind, really — she's always been; but I probably didn't explain it right. I do wish I could find some place for you, though!"

The boy shrugged his shoulders and half turned away.

"Never mind. I guess I can find one myself. I ain't no beggar, you know."

Pollyanna was frowning thoughtfully. Of a sudden she turned, her face illumined.

"Say, I'll tell you what I *will* do! The Ladies'

Aid meets this afternoon. I heard Aunt Polly say so. I'll lay your case before them. That's what father always did, when he wanted anything — educating the heathen and new carpets, you know."

The boy turned fiercely.

"Well, I ain't a heathen or a new carpet. Besides — what is a Ladies' Aid?"

Pollyanna stared in shocked disapproval.

"Why, Jimmy Bean, wherever have you been brought up? — not to know what a Ladies' Aid is!"

"Oh, all right — if you ain't tellin'," grunted the boy, turning and beginning to walk away indifferently.

Pollyanna sprang to his side at once.

"It's — it's — why, it's just a lot of ladies that meet and sew and give suppers and raise money and — and talk; that's what a Ladies' Aid is. They're awfully kind — that is, most of mine was, back home. I haven't seen this one here, but they're always good, I reckon. I'm going to tell them about you this afternoon."

Again the boy turned fiercely.

"Not much you will! Maybe you think I'm goin' ter stand 'round an' hear a whole *lot* o' women call me a beggar, instead of jest *one!* Not much!"

"Oh, but you wouldn't be there," argued Pollyanna, quickly. "I'd go alone, of course, and tell
them."

"You would?"

"Yes; and I'd tell it better this time," hurried
on Pollyanna, quick to see the signs of relenting in
the boy's face. "And there'd be some of 'em, I
know, that would be glad to give you a home."

"I'd work — don't forget ter say that," cau-
tioned the boy.

"Of course not," promised Pollyanna, happily,
sure now that her point was gained. "Then I'll let
you know to-morrow."

"Where?"

"By the road — where I found you to-day; near
Mrs. Snow's house."

"All right. I'll be there." The boy paused before he went on slowly: "Maybe I'd better go back,
then, for ter-night, ter the Home. You see I hain't
no other place ter stay; and — and I didn't leave
till this mornin'. I slipped out. I didn't tell 'em I
wasn't comin' back, else they'd pretend I couldn't
come — though I'm thinkin' they won't do no
worryin' when I don't show up sometime. They
ain't like *folks*, ye know. They don't *care!*"

"I know," nodded Pollyanna, with understand-

ing eyes. " But I'm sure, when I see you to-morrow, I'll have just a common home and folks that
do care all ready for you. Good-by!" she called
brightly, as she turned back toward the house.

In the sitting-room window at that moment, Miss
Polly, who had been watching the two children,
followed with sombre eyes the boy until a bend of
the road hid him from sight. Then she sighed,
turned, and walked listlesly up-stairs — and Miss
Polly did not usually move listlessly. In her ears
still was the boy's scornful "you was so good and
kind." In her heart was a curious sense of desola-
tion — as of something lost,

CHAPTER XII

BEFORE THE LADIES' AID

DINNER, which came at noon in the Harrington homestead, was a silent meal on the day of the Ladies' Aid meeting. Pollyanna, it is true, tried to talk; but she did not make a success of it, chiefly because four times she was obliged to break off a " glad " in the middle of it, much to her blushing discomfort. The fifth time it happened, Miss Polly moved her head wearily.

" There, there, child, say it, if you want to," she sighed. " I'm sure I'd rather you did than not — if it's going to make all this fuss."

Pollyanna's puckered little face cleared.

" Oh, thank you. I'm afraid it would be pretty hard — not to say it. You see I've played it so long."

" You've — what?" demanded Aunt Polly.

" Played it — the game, you know, that father — " Pollyanna stopped with a painful blush at finding herself so soon again on forbidden ground.

Aunt Polly frowned and said nothing. The rest of the meal was a silent one.

Pollyanna was not sorry to hear Aunt Polly tell the minister's wife over the telephone, a little later, that she would not be at the Ladies' Aid meeting that afternoon, owing to a headache. When Aunt Polly went up-stairs to her room and closed the door, Pollyanna tried to be sorry for the headache; but she could not help feeling glad that her aunt was not to be present that afternoon when she laid the case of Jimmy Bean before the Ladies' Aid. She could not forget that Aunt Polly had called Jimmy Bean a little beggar; and she did not want Aunt Polly to call him that — before the Ladies' Aid.

Pollyanna knew that the Ladies' Aid met at two o'clock in the chapel next the church, not quite half a mile from home. She planned her going, therefore, so that she should get there a little before three.

" I want them all to be there," she said to herself; " else the very one that wasn't there might be the one who would be wanting to give Jimmy Bean a home; and, of course, two o'clock always means three, really — to Ladies' Aiders."

Quietly, but with confident courage, Pollyanna

ascended the chapel steps, pushed open the door and entered the vestibule. A soft babel of feminine chatter and laughter came from the main room. Hesitating only a brief moment Pollyanna pushed open one of the inner doors.

The chatter dropped to a surprised hush. Pollyanna advanced a little timidly. Now that the time had come, she felt unwontedly shy. After all, these half-strange, half-familiar faces about her were not her own dear Ladies' Aid.

"How do you do, Ladies' Aiders?" she faltered politely. "I'm Pollyanna Whittier. I — I reckon some of you know me, maybe; anyway, I do *you* — only I don't know you all together this way."

The silence could almost be felt now. Some of the ladies did know this rather extraordinary niece of their fellow-member, and nearly all had heard of her; but not one of them could think of anything to say, just then.

"I — I've come to — to lay the case before you," stammered Pollyanna, after a moment, unconsciously falling into her father's familiar phraseology.

There was a slight rustle.

"Did — did your aunt send you, my dear?" asked Mrs. Ford, the minister's wife.

Pollyanna colored a little.

" Oh, no. I came all by myself. You see, I'm used to Ladies' Aiders. It was Ladies' Aiders that brought me up — with father."

Somebody tittered hysterically, and the minister's wife frowned.

" Yes, dear. What is it? "

" Well, it — it's Jimmy Bean," sighed Pollyanna. " He hasn't any home except the Orphan one, and they're full, and don't want him, anyhow, he thinks; so he wants another. He wants one of the common kind, that has a mother instead of a Matron in it — folks, you know, that'll care. He's ten years old going on eleven. I thought some of you might like him — to live with you, you know."

" Well, did you ever! " murmured a voice, breaking the dazed pause that followed Pollyanna's words.

With anxious eyes Pollyanna swept the circle of faces about her.

" Oh, I forgot to say; he will work," she supplemented eagerly.

Still there was silence; then, coldly, one or two women began to question her. After a time they all had the story and began to talk among themselves, animatedly, not quite pleasantly.

Pollyanna listened with growing anxiety. Some of what was said she could not understand. She did gather, after a time, however, that there was no woman there who had a home to give him, though every woman seemed to think that some of the others might take him, as there were several who had no little boys of their own already in their homes. But there was no one who agreed herself to take him. Then she heard the minister's wife suggest timidly that they, as a society, might perhaps assume his support and education instead of sending quite so much money this year to the little boys in far-away India.

A great many ladies talked then, and several of them talked all at once, and even more loudly and more unpleasantly than before. It seemed that their society was famous for its offering to Hindu missions, and several said they should die of mortification if it should be less this year. Some of what was said at this time Pollyanna again thought she could not have understood, too, for it sounded almost as if they did not care at all what the money *did*, so long as the sum opposite the name of their society in a certain " report " " headed the list " — and of course that could not be what they meant at all! But it was all very confusing, and not quite pleasant, so that Pollyanna was glad, indeed, when at last she found herself outside in the hushed, sweet air — only she was very sorry, too: for she knew it was not going to be easy, or anything but sad, to tell Jimmy Bean to-morrow that the Ladies' Aid had decided that they would rather send all their money to bring up the little India boys than to save out enough to bring up one little boy in their own town, for which they would not get "a bit of credit in the report," according to the tall lady who wore spectacles.

"Not but that it's good, of course, to send money to the heathen, and I shouldn't want 'em not to send *some* there," sighed Pollyanna to herself, as she trudged sorrowfully along. "But they acted as if little boys *here* weren't any account — only little boys 'way off. I should *think*, though, they'd rather see Jimmy Bean grow — than just a report!"

CHAPTER XIII

IN PENDLETON WOODS

POLLYANNA had not turned her steps toward home, when she left the chapel. She had turned them, instead, toward Pendleton Hill. It had been a hard day, for all it had been a " vacation one " (as she termed the infrequent days when there was no sewing or cooking lesson), and Pollyanna was sure that nothing would do her quite so much good as a walk through the green quiet of Pendleton Woods. Up Pendleton Hill, therefore, she climbed steadily, in spite of the warm sun on her back.

" I don't have to get home till half-past five, anyway," she was telling herself; " and it'll be so much nicer to go around by the way of the woods, even if I do have to climb to get there."

It was very beautiful in the Pendleton Woods, as Pollyanna knew by experience. But to-day it seemed even more delightful than ever, notwithstanding her disappointment over what she must tell Jimmy Bean to-morrow.

"I wish they were up here — all those ladies who talked so loud," sighed Pollyanna to herself, raising her eyes to the patches of vivid blue between the sunlit green of the tree-tops. "Anyhow, if they were up here, I just reckon they'd change and take Jimmy Bean for their little boy, all right," she finished, secure in her conviction, but unable to give a reason for it, even to herself.

Suddenly Pollyanna lifted her head and listened. A dog had barked some distance ahead. A moment later he came dashing toward her, still barking.

"Hullo, doggie — hullo!" Pollyanna snapped her fingers at the dog and looked expectantly down the path. She had seen the dog once before, she was sure. He had been then with the Man, Mr. John Pendleton. She was looking now, hoping to see him. For some minutes she watched eagerly, but he did not appear. Then she turned her attention toward the dog.

The dog, as even Pollyanna could see, was acting strangely. He was still barking — giving little short, sharp yelps, as if of alarm. He was running back and forth, too, in the path ahead. Soon they reached a side path, and down this the little dog fairly flew, only to come back at once, whining and barking.

"Ho! That isn't the way home," laughed Pollyanna, still keeping to the main path.

The little dog seemed frantic now. Back and forth, back and forth, between Pollyanna and the side path he vibrated, barking and whining pitifully. Every quiver of his little brown body, and every glance from his beseeching brown eyes were eloquent with appeal — so eloquent that at last Pollyanna understood, turned, and followed him.

Straight ahead, now, the little dog dashed madly; and it was not long before Pollyanna came upon the reason for it all: a man lying motionless at the foot of a steep, overhanging mass of rock a few yards from the side path.

A twig cracked sharply under Pollyanna's foot, and the man turned his head. With a cry of dismay Pollyanna ran to his side.

"Mr. Pendleton! Oh, are you hurt?"

"Hurt? Oh, no! I'm just taking a siesta in the sunshine," snapped the man irritably. "See here, how much do you know? What can you do? Have you got any sense?"

Pollyanna caught her breath with a little gasp, but — as was her habit — she answered the questions literally, one by one.

"Why, Mr. Pendleton, I — I don't know so very

much, and I can't do a great many things; but
most of the Ladies' Aiders, except Mrs. Rawson,
said I had real good sense. I heard 'em say so one
day — they didn't know I heard, though."

The man smiled grimly.

"There, there, child, I beg your pardon, I'm
sure; it's only this confounded leg of mine. Now
listen." He paused, and with some difficulty
reached his hand into his trousers pocket and
brought out a bunch of keys, singling out one between his thumb and forefinger. "Straight
through the path there, about five minutes' walk, is
my house. This key will admit you to the side door
under the porte-cochère. Do you know what a
porte-cochère is?"

"Oh, yes, sir. Auntie has one with a sun parlor
over it. That's the roof I slept on — only I didn't
sleep, you know. They found me."

"Eh? Oh! Well, when you get into the house,
go straight through the vestibule and hall to the
door at the end. On the big, flat-topped desk in
the middle of the room you'll find a telephone. Do
you know how to use a telephone?"

"Oh, yes, sir! Why, once when Aunt Polly — "

"Never mind Aunt Polly now," cut in the man
scowlingly, as he tried to move himself a little.

"Hunt up Dr. Thomas Chilton's number on the card you'll find somewhere around there — it ought to be on the hook down at the side, but it probably won't be. You know a telephone card, I suppose, when you see one!"

"Oh, yes, sir! I just love Aunt Polly's. There's such a lot of queer names, and — "

"Tell Dr. Chilton that John Pendleton is at the foot of Little Eagle Ledge in Pendleton Woods with a broken leg, and to come at once with a stretcher and two men. He'll know what to do besides that. Tell him to come by the path from the house."

"A broken leg? Oh, Mr. Pendleton, how perfectly awful!" shuddered Pollyanna. "But I'm so glad I came! Can't *I* do — "

" Yes, you can — but evidently you won't! *Will* you go and do what I ask and stop talking," moaned the man, faintly. And, with a little sobbing cry, Pollyanna went.

Pollyanna did not stop now to look up at the patches of blue between the sunlit tops of the trees. She kept her eyes on the ground to make sure that no twig nor stone tripped her hurrying feet.

It was not long before she came in sight of the house. She had seen it before, though never so

near as this. She was almost frightened now at
the massiveness of the great pile of gray stone with
its pillared verandas and its imposing entrance.
Pausing only a moment, however, she sped across
the big neglected lawn and around the house to the
side door under the porte-cochère. Her fingers,
stiff from their tight clutch upon the keys, were anything but skilful in their efforts to turn the bolt in
the lock; but at last the heavy, carved door swung
slowly back on its hinges.

Pollyanna caught her breath. In spite of her
feeling of haste, she paused a moment and looked
fearfully through the vestibule to the wide, sombre
hall beyond, her thoughts in a whirl. This was
John Pendleton's house; the house of mystery; the
house into which no one but its master entered; the
house which sheltered, somewhere — a skeleton.
Yet she, Pollyanna, was expected to enter alone
these fearsome rooms, and telephone the doctor that
the master of the house lay now —

With a little cry Pollyanna, looking neither to
the right nor the left, fairly ran through the hall
to the door at the end and opened it.

The room was large, and sombre with dark woods
and hangings like the hall; but through the west
window the sun threw a long shaft of gold across

the floor, gleamed dully on the tarnished brass and-irons in the fireplace, and touched the nickel of the telephone on the great desk in the middle of the room. It was toward this desk that Pollyanna hurriedly tiptoed.

The telephone card was not on its hook; it was on the floor. But Pollyanna found it, and ran her shaking forefinger down through the C's to " Chilton." In due time she had Dr. Chilton himself at the other end of the wires, and was tremblingly delivering her message and answering the doctor's terse, pertinent questions. This done, she hung up the receiver and drew a long breath of relief.

Only a brief glance did Pollyanna give about her; then, with a confused vision in her eyes of crimson draperies, book-lined walls, a littered floor, an untidy desk, innumerable closed doors (any one of which might conceal a skeleton), and everywhere dust, dust, dust, she fled back through the hall to the great carved door, still half open as she had left it.

In what seemed, even to the injured man, an incredibly short time, Pollyanna was back in the woods at the man's side.

" Well, what is the trouble? Couldn't you get in? " he demanded.

Pollyanna opened wide her eyes.

"Why, of course I could! I'm *here*," she answered. "As if I'd be here if I hadn't got in! And the doctor will be right up just as soon as possible with the men and things. He said he knew just where you were, so I didn't stay to show him. I wanted to be with you."

"Did you?" smiled the man, grimly. "Well, I can't say I admire your taste. I should think you might find pleasanter companions."

"Do you mean — because you're so — cross?"

"Thanks for your frankness. Yes."

Pollyanna laughed softly.

"But you're only cross *outside* — you aren't cross inside a bit!"

"Indeed! How do you know that?" asked the man, trying to change the position of his head without moving the rest of his body.

"Oh, lots of ways; there — like that — the way you act with the dog," she added, pointing to the long, slender hand that rested on the dog's sleek head near him. "It's funny how dogs and cats know the insides of folks better than other folks do, isn't it? Say, I'm going to hold your head," she finished abruptly.

The man winced several times and groaned once

softly while the change was being made; but in the end he found Pollyanna's lap a very welcome substitute for the rocky hollow in which his head had lain before.

" Well, that is — better," he murmured faintly.

He did not speak again for some time. Pollyanna, watching his face, wondered if he were asleep. She did not think he was. He looked as if his lips were tight shut to keep back moans of pain. Pollyanna herself almost cried aloud as she looked at his great, strong body lying there so helpless. One hand, with fingers tightly clenched, lay outflung, motionless. The other, limply open, lay on the dog's head. The dog, his wistful, eager eyes on his master's face, was motionless, too.

Minute by minute the time passed. The sun dropped lower in the west and the shadows grew deeper under the trees. Pollyanna sat so still she hardly seemed to breathe. A bird alighted fearlessly within reach of her hand, and a squirrel whisked his bushy tail on a tree-branch almost under her nose — yet with his bright little eyes all the while on the motionless dog.

At last the dog pricked up his ears and whined softly; then he gave a short, sharp bark. The next moment Pollyanna heard voices, and very soon their owners appeared — three men carrying a stretcher and various other articles.

The tallest of the party — a smooth-shaven, kind-eyed man whom Pollyanna knew by sight as "Dr. Chilton" — advanced cheerily.

"Well, my little lady, playing nurse?"

"Oh, no, sir," smiled Pollyanna. "I've only held his head — I haven't given him a mite of medicine. But I'm glad I was here."

"So am I," nodded the doctor, as he turned his absorbed attention to the injured man.

CHAPTER XIV

JUST A MATTER OF JELLY

POLLYANNA was a little late for supper on the night of the accident to John Pendleton; but, as it happened, she escaped without reproof.

Nancy met her at the door.

"Well, if I ain't glad ter be settin' my two eyes on you," she sighed in obvious relief. "It's half-past six!"

"I know it," admitted Pollyanna anxiously; "but I'm not to blame — truly I'm not. And I don't think even Aunt Polly will say I am, either."

"She won't have the chance," retorted Nancy, with huge satisfaction. "She's gone."

"Gone!" gasped Pollyanna. "You don't mean that I've driven her away?" Through Pollyanna's mind at the moment trooped remorseful memories of the morning with its unwanted boy, cat, and dog, and its unwelcome "glad" and forbidden "father" that would spring to her forgetful little tongue. "Oh, I *didn't* drive her away?"

138

"Not much you did," scoffed Nancy. "Her cousin died suddenly down to Boston, and she had ter go. She had one o' them yeller telegram letters after you went away this afternoon, and she won't be back for three days. Now I guess we're glad all right. We'll be keepin' house tergether, jest you and me, all that time. We will, we will!"

Pollyanna looked shocked.

"Glad! Oh, Nancy, when it's a funeral?"

"Oh, but 'twa'n't the funeral I was glad for, Miss Pollyanna. It was —" Nancy stopped abruptly. A shrewd twinkle came into her eyes. "Why, Miss Pollyanna, as if it wa'n't yerself that was teachin' me ter play the game," she reproached her gravely.

Pollyanna puckered her forehead into a troubled frown.

"I can't help it, Nancy," she argued with a shake of her head. "It must be that there are some things that 'tisn't right to play the game on — and I'm sure funerals is one of them. There's nothing in a funeral to be glad about."

Nancy chuckled.

"We can be glad 'tain't our'n," she observed demurely. But Pollyanna did not hear. She had begun to tell of the accident; and in a moment Nancy, open-mouthed, was listening.

At the appointed place the next afternoon, Polly-anna met Jimmy Bean according to agreement. As was to be expected, of course, Jimmy showed keen disappointment that the Ladies' Aid preferred a little India boy to himself.

"Well, maybe 'tis natural," he sighed. "Of course things you don't know about are always nicer'n things you do, same as the pertater on 'tother side of the plate is always the biggest. But I wish I looked that way ter somebody 'way off. Wouldn't it be jest great, now, if only somebody over in India wanted *me?*"

Pollyanna clapped her hands.

"Why, of course! That's the very thing, Jimmy! I'll write to *my* Ladies' Aiders about you. They aren't over in India; they're only out West — but that's awful far away, just the same. I reckon you'd think so if you'd come all the way here as I did!"

Jimmy's face brightened.

"Do you think they would — truly — take me?" he asked.

"Of course they would! Don't they take little boys in India to bring up? Well, they can just play you are the little India boy this time. I reckon you're far enough away to make a report, all right.

You wait. I'll write 'em. I'll write Mrs. White. No, I'll write Mrs. Jones. Mrs. White has got the most money, but Mrs. Jones gives the most — which is kind of funny, isn't it? — when you think of it. But I reckon some of the Aiders will take you."

"All right — but don't furgit ter say I'll work fur my board an' keep," put in Jimmy. "I ain't no beggar, an' biz'ness is biz'ness, even with Ladies' Aiders, I'm thinkin'." He hesitated, then added: "An' I s'pose I better stay where I be fur a spell yet — till you hear."

"Of course," nodded Pollyanna emphatically. "Then I'll know just where to find you. And they'll take you — I'm sure you're far enough away for that. Didn't Aunt Polly take — Say!" she broke off, suddenly, "*do* you suppose I was Aunt Polly's little girl from India?"

"Well, if you ain't the queerest kid," grinned Jimmy, as he turned away.

It was about a week after the accident in Pendleton Woods that Pollyanna said to her aunt one morning:

"Aunt Polly, please would you mind very much if I took Mrs. Snow's calf's-foot jelly this week to some one else? I'm sure Mrs. Snow wouldn't — this once."

" Dear me, Pollyanna, what *are* you up to now?"
sighed her aunt. " You *are* the most extraordinary
child!"

Pollyanna frowned a little anxiously.

" Aunt Polly, please, what is extraordinary? If
you're *ex*traordinary you can't be *or*dinary, can
you?"

" You certainly can not."

" Oh, that's all right, then. I'm glad I'm *ex*-
traordinary," sighed Pollyanna, her face clearing.
" You see, Mrs. White used to say Mrs. Rawson
was a very ordinary woman — and she disliked
Mrs. Rawson something awful. They were always
fight— I mean, father had — that is, I mean, *we*
had more trouble keeping peace between them than
we did between any of the rest of the Aiders," corrected Pollyanna, a little breathless from her efforts
to steer between the Scylla of her father's past
commands in regard to speaking of church quarrels,
and the Charybdis of her aunt's present commands
in regard to speaking of her father.

" Yes, yes; well, never mind," interposed Aunt
Polly, a trifle impatiently. " You do run on so,
Pollyanna, and no matter what we're talking about
you always bring up at those Ladies' Aiders!"

" Yes'm," smiled Pollyanna, cheerfully, " I

reckon I do, maybe. But you see they used to bring me up, and — ”

“ That will do, Pollyanna,” interrupted a cold voice. “ Now what is it about this jelly? ”

“ Nothing, Aunt Polly, truly, that you would mind, I’m sure. You let me take jelly to *her,* so I thought you would to *him* — this once. You see, broken legs aren’t like — like lifelong invalids, so his won’t last forever as Mrs. Snow’s does, and *she* can have all the rest of the things after just once or twice.”

“ ‘ Him ’? ‘ He ’? ‘ Broken leg ’? What are you talking about, Pollyanna? ”

Pollyanna stared; then her face relaxed.

“ Oh, I forgot. I reckon you didn’t know. You see, it happened while you were gone. It was the very day you went that I found him in the woods, you know; and I had to unlock his house and telephone for the men and the doctor, and hold his head, and everything. And of course then I came away and haven’t seen him since. But when Nancy made the jelly for Mrs. Snow this week I thought how nice it would be if I could take it to him instead of her, just this once. Aunt Polly, may I? ”

“ Yes, yes, I suppose so,” acquiesced Miss Polly, a little wearily. “ Who did you say he was? ”

" The Man. I mean, Mr. John Pendleton."

Miss Polly almost sprang from her chair.

" *John Pendleton!* "

" Yes. Nancy told me his name. Maybe you know him."

Miss Polly did not answer this. Instead she asked:

" Do *you* know him? "

Pollyanna nodded.

" Oh, yes. He always speaks and smiles — now. He's only cross *outside,* you know. I'll go and get the jelly. Nancy had it 'most fixed when I came in," finished Pollyanna, already halfway across the room.

" Pollyanna, wait! " Miss Polly's voice was suddenly very stern. " I've changed my mind. I would prefer that Mrs. Snow had that jelly to-day — as usual. That is all. You may go now."

Pollyanna's face fell.

" Oh, but Aunt Polly, *hers* will last. She can always be sick and have things, you know; but *his* is just a broken leg, and legs don't last — I mean, broken ones. He's had it a whole week now."

" Yes, I remember. I heard Mr. John Pendleton had met with an accident," said Miss Polly, a little stiffly; "but — I do not care to be sending jelly to John Pendleton, Pollyanna."

"I know, he is cross — outside," admitted Pollyanna, sadly, "so I suppose you don't like him. But I wouldn't say 'twas you sent it. I'd say 'twas me. I like him. I'd be glad to send him jelly."

Miss Polly began to shake her head again. Then, suddenly, she stopped, and asked in a curiously quiet voice:

"Does he know who you — are, Pollyanna?"

The little girl sighed.

"I reckon not. I told him my name, once, but he never calls me it — never."

"Does he know where you — live?"

"Oh, no. I never told him that."

"Then he doesn't know you're my — niece?"

"I don't think so."

For a moment there was silence. Miss Polly was looking at Pollyanna with eyes that did not seem to see her at all. The little girl, shifting impatiently from one small foot to the other, sighed audibly. Then Miss Polly roused herself with a start.

"Very well, Pollyanna," she said at last, still in that queer voice, so unlike her own; "you may — you may take the jelly to Mr. Pendleton as your

own gift. But understand: I do not send it. Be
very sure that he does not think I do!"

"Yes'm — no'm — thank you, Aunt Polly," exulted Pollyanna, as she flew through the door.

CHAPTER XV

DR. CHILTON

THE great gray pile of masonry looked very different to Pollyanna when she made her second visit to the house of Mr. John Pendleton. Windows were open, an elderly woman was hanging out clothes in the back yard, and the doctor's gig stood under the porte-cochère.

As before Pollyanna went to the side door. This time she rang the bell — her fingers were not stiff to-day from a tight clutch on a bunch of keys.

A familiar-looking small dog bounded up the steps to greet her, but there was a slight delay before the woman who had been hanging out the clothes opened the door.

"If you please, I've brought some calf's-foot jelly for Mr. Pendleton," smiled Pollyanna.

"Thank you," said the woman, reaching for the bowl in the little girl's hand. "Who shall I say sent it? And it's calf's-foot jelly?"

The doctor, coming into the hall at that moment,

heard the woman's words and saw the disappointed look on Pollyanna's face. He stepped quickly forward.

"Ah! Some calf's-foot jelly?" he asked genially. "That will be fine! Maybe you'd like to see our patient, eh?"

"Oh, yes, sir," beamed Pollyanna; and the woman, in obedience to a nod from the doctor, led the way down the hall at once, though plainly with vast surprise on her face.

Behind the doctor, a young man (a trained nurse from the nearest city) gave a disturbed exclamation.

"But, Doctor, didn't Mr. Pendleton give orders not to admit — any one?"

"Oh, yes," nodded the doctor, imperturbably. "But I'm giving orders now. I'll take the risk." Then he added whimsically: "You don't know, of course; but that little girl is better than a six-quart bottle of tonic any day. If anything or anybody can take the grouch out of Pendleton this afternoon, she can. That's why I sent her in."

"Who is she?"

For one brief moment the doctor hesitated.

"She's the niece of one of our best known residents. Her name is Pollyanna Whittier. I — I don't happen to enjoy a very extensive personal ac-

quaintance with the little lady as yet; but lots of
my patients do — I'm thankful to say!"

The nurse smiled.

"Indeed! And what are the special ingredients
of this wonder-working — tonic of hers?"

The doctor shook his head.

"I don't know. As near as I can find out it is
an overwhelming, unquenchable gladness for everything that has happened or is going to happen. At
any rate, her quaint speeches are constantly being
repeated to me, and, as near as I can make out,
'just being glad' is the tenor of most of them.
All is," he added, with another whimsical smile, as
he stepped out on to the porch, "I wish I could
prescribe her — and buy her — as I would a box
of pills; — though if there gets to be many of her
in the world, you and I might as well go to ribbon-
selling and ditch-digging for all the money we'd
get out of nursing and doctoring," he laughed, picking up the reins and stepping into the gig.

Pollyanna, meanwhile, in accordance with the
doctor's orders, was being escorted to John Pendleton's rooms.

Her way led through the great library at the end
of the hall, and, rapid as was her progress through
it, Pollyanna saw at once that great changes had

taken place. The book-lined walls and the crimson curtains were the same; but there was no litter on the floor, no untidiness on the desk, and not so much as a grain of dust in sight. The telephone card hung in its proper place, and the brass andirons had been polished. One of the mysterious doors was open, and it was toward this that the maid led the way. A moment later Pollyanna found herself in a sumptuously furnished bedroom while the maid was saying in a frightened voice:

" If you please, sir, here — here's a little girl with some jelly. The doctor said I was to — to bring her in."

The next moment Pollyanna found herself alone with a very cross-looking man lying flat on his back in bed.

" See here, didn't I say — " began an angry voice. " Oh, it's you!" it broke off not very graciously, as Pollyanna advanced toward the bed.

" Yes, sir," smiled Pollyanna. " Oh, I'm so glad they let me in! You see, at first the lady 'most took my jelly, and I was so afraid I wasn't going to see you at all. Then the doctor came, and he said I might. Wasn't he lovely to let me see you?"

In spite of himself the man's lips twitched into a smile; but all he said was " Humph!"

"And I've brought you some jelly," resumed Pollyanna; "— calf's-foot. I hope you like it?" There was a rising inflection in her voice.

"Never ate it." The fleeting smile had gone, and the scowl had come back to the man's face.

For a brief instant Pollyanna's countenance showed disappointment; but it cleared as she set the bowl of jelly down.

"Didn't you? Well, if you didn't, then you can't know you *don't* like it, anyhow, can you? So I reckon I'm glad you haven't, after all. Now, if you knew —"

"Yes, yes; well, there's one thing I know all right, and that is that I'm flat on my back right here this minute, and that I'm liable to stay here — till doomsday, I guess."

Pollyanna looked shocked.

"Oh, no! It couldn't be till doomsday, you know, when the angel Gabriel blows his trumpet, unless it should come quicker than we think it will — oh, of course, I know the Bible says it may come quicker than we think, but I don't think it will — that is, of course I believe the Bible; but I mean I don't think it will come as much quicker as it would if it should come now, and —"

John Pendleton laughed suddenly — and aloud.

The nurse, coming in at that moment, heard the laugh, and beat a hurried — but a very silent — retreat. He had the air of a frightened cook who, seeing the danger of a breath of cold air striking a half-done cake, hastily shuts the oven door.

" Aren't you getting a little mixed? " asked John Pendleton of Pollyanna.

The little girl laughed.

" Maybe. But what I mean is, that legs don't last — broken ones, you know — like lifelong invalids, same as Mrs. Snow has got. So yours won't last till doomsday at all. I should think you could be glad of that."

" Oh, I am," retorted the man grimly.

" And you didn't break but one. You can be glad 'twasn't two." Pollyanna was warming to her task.

" Of course! So fortunate," sniffed the man, with uplifted eyebrows; " looking at it from that standpoint, I suppose I might be glad I wasn't a centipede and didn't break fifty! "

Pollyanna chuckled.

" Oh, that's the best yet," she crowed. " I know what a centipede is; they've got lots of legs. And you can be glad — "

" Oh, of course," interrupted the man, sharply, all the old bitterness coming back to his voice; " I

can be glad, too, for all the rest, I suppose — the
nurse, and the doctor, and that confounded woman
in the kitchen!"

"Why, yes, sir — only think how bad 'twould be
if you *didn't* have them!"

"Well, I — eh?" he demanded sharply.

"Why, I say, only think how bad it would be if
you didn't have 'em — and you lying here like
this!"

"As if that wasn't the very thing that was at the
bottom of the whole matter," retorted the man,
testily, "because I *am* lying here like this! And
yet you expect me to say I'm glad because of a fool
woman who disarranges the whole house and calls
it 'regulating,' and a man who aids and abets her
in it, and calls it 'nursing,' to say nothing of the
doctor who eggs 'em both on — and the whole
bunch of them, meanwhile, expecting me to pay
them for it, and pay them well, too!"

Pollyanna frowned sympathetically.

"Yes, I know. *That* part is too bad — about
the money — when you've been saving it, too, all
this time."

"When — eh?"

"Saving it — buying beans and fish balls, you
know. Say, *do* you like beans? — or do *you*

like turkey better, only on account of the sixty
cents?"

"Look a-here, child, what are you talking
about?"

Pollyanna smiled radiantly.

"About your money, you know — denying yourself, and saving it for the heathen. You see, I
found out about it. Why, Mr. Pendleton, that's
one of the ways I knew you weren't cross inside.
Nancy told me."

The man's jaw dropped.

"Nancy told you I was saving money for the —
Well, may I inquire who Nancy is?"

"Our Nancy. She works for Aunt Polly."

"Aunt Polly! Well, who is Aunt Polly?"

"She's Miss Polly Harrington. I live with her."

The man made a sudden movement.

"Miss — Polly — Harrington!" he breathed.
"You live with — *her!*"

"Yes; I'm her niece. She's taken me to bring
up — on account of my mother, you know," faltered Pollyanna, in a low voice. "She was her
sister. And after father — went to be with her and
the rest of us in Heaven, there wasn't any one left
for me down here but the Ladies' Aid; so she took
me."

The man did not answer. His face, as he lay back on the pillow now, was very white — so white that Pollyanna was frightened. She rose uncertainly to her feet.

"I reckon maybe I'd better go now," she proposed. "I — I hope you'll like — the jelly."

The man turned his head suddenly, and opened his eyes. There was a curious longing in their dark depths which even Pollyanna saw, and at which she marvelled.

"And so you are — Miss Polly Harrington's niece," he said gently.

"Yes, sir."

Still the man's dark eyes lingered on her face, until Pollyanna, feeling vaguely restless, murmured:

"I — I suppose you know — her."

John Pendleton's lips curved in an odd smile.

"Oh, yes; I know her." He hesitated, then went on, still with that curious smile. "But — you don't mean — you can't mean that it was Miss Polly Harrington who sent that jelly — to me?" he said slowly.

Pollyanna looked distressed.

"N-no, sir; she didn't. She said I must be very sure not to let you think she did send it. But I —"

"I thought as much," vouchsafed the man, shortly, turning away his head. And Pollyanna, still more distressed, tiptoed from the room.

Under the porte-cochère she found the doctor waiting in his gig. The nurse stood on the steps.

"Well, Miss Pollyanna, may I have the pleasure of seeing you home?" asked the doctor smilingly. "I started to drive on a few minutes ago; then it occurred to me that I'd wait for you."

"Thank you, sir. I'm glad you did. I just love to ride," beamed Pollyanna, as he reached out his hand to help her in.

"Do you?" smiled the doctor, nodding his head in farewell to the young man on the steps. "Well, as near as I can judge, there are a good many things you 'love' to do — eh?" he added, as they drove briskly away.

Pollyanna laughed.

"Why, I don't know. I reckon perhaps there are," she admitted. "I like to do 'most everything that's *living*. Of course I don't like the other things very well — sewing, and reading out loud, and all that. But *they* aren't *living*."

"No? What are they, then?"

"Aunt Polly says they're 'learning to live,'" sighed Pollyanna, with a rueful smile.

The doctor smiled now — a little queerly.

"Does she? Well, I should think she might say — just that."

"Yes," responded Pollyanna. "But I don't see it that way at all. I don't think you have to *learn* how to live. I didn't, anyhow."

The doctor drew a long sigh.

"After all, I'm afraid some of us — do have to, little girl," he said. Then, for a time he was silent. Pollyanna, stealing a glance at his face, felt vaguely sorry for him. He looked so sad. She wished, uneasily, that she could "do something." It was this, perhaps, that caused her to say in a timid voice:

"Dr. Chilton, I should think being a doctor would be the very gladdest kind of a business there was."

The doctor turned in surprise.

"'Gladdest'! — when I see so much suffering always, everywhere I go?" he cried.

She nodded.

"I know; but you're *helping* it — don't you see? — and of course you're glad to help it! And so that makes you the gladdest of any of us, all the time."

The doctor's eyes filled with sudden hot tears. The doctor's life was a singularly lonely one. He had no wife and no home save his two-room office in a boarding house. His profession was very dear to him. Looking now into Pollyanna's shining eyes, he felt as if a loving hand had been suddenly laid on his head in blessing. He knew, too, that never again would a long day's work or a long night's weariness be quite without that new-found exaltation that had come to him through Pollyanna's eyes.

"God bless you, little girl," he said unsteadily. Then, with the bright smile his patients knew and loved so well, he added: "And I'm thinking, after all, that it was the doctor, quite as much as his patients, that needed a draft of that tonic!" All of which puzzled Pollyanna very much — until a chipmunk, running across the road, drove the whole matter from her mind.

The doctor left Pollyanna at her own door, smiled at Nancy, who was sweeping off the front porch, then drove rapidly away.

"I've had a perfectly beautiful ride with the doctor," announced Pollyanna, bounding up the steps. "He's lovely, Nancy!"

"Is he?"

"Yes. And I told him I should think his business would be the very gladdest one there was."

"What!—goin' ter see sick folks—an' folks what ain't sick but thinks they is, which is worse?" Nancy's face showed open skepticism.

Pollyanna laughed gleefully.

"Yes. That's 'most what he said, too; but there is a way to be glad, even then. Guess!"

Nancy frowned in meditation. Nancy was getting so she could play this game of "being glad" quite successfully, she thought. She rather enjoyed studying out Pollyanna's "posers," too, as she called some of the little girl's questions.

"Oh, I know," she chuckled. "It's just the opposite from what you told Mis' Snow."

"Opposite?" repeated Pollyanna, obviously puzzled.

"Yes. You told her she could be glad because other folks wasn't like her—all sick, you know."

"Yes," nodded Pollyanna.

"Well, the doctor can be glad because *he* isn't like other folks—the sick ones, I mean, what he doctors," finished Nancy in triumph.

It was Pollyanna's turn to frown.

"Why, y-yes," she admitted. "Of course that *is* one way, but it isn't the way I said; and—someway, I don't seem to quite like the sound of it. It isn't exactly as if he said he was glad they *were* sick, but — You do play the game so funny, sometimes, Nancy," she sighed, as she went into the house.

Pollyanna found her aunt in the sitting room.

" Who was that man — the one who drove into the yard, Pollyanna?" questioned the lady a little sharply.

" Why, Aunt Polly, that was Dr. Chilton! Don't you know him?"

" Dr. Chilton! What was he doing — here?"

" He drove me home. Oh, and I gave the jelly to Mr. Pendleton, and — "

Miss Polly lifted her head quickly.

" Pollyanna, he did not think I sent it?"

" Oh, no, Aunt Polly. I told him you didn't."

Miss Polly grew a sudden vivid pink.

" You *told* him I didn't!"

Pollyanna opened wide her eyes at the remonstrative dismay in her aunt's voice.

" Why, Aunt Polly, you *said* to!"

Aunt Polly sighed.

" I *said*, Pollyanna, that I did not send it, and for you to be very sure that he did not think I *did!* — which is a very different matter from *telling* him outright that I did not send it." And she turned vexedly away.

" Dear me! Well, I don't see where the difference is," sighed Pollyanna, as she went to hang her hat on the one particular hook in the house upon which Aunt Polly had said that it must be hung.

CHAPTER XVI

A RED ROSE AND A LACE SHAWL

IT was on a rainy day about a week after Pollyanna's visit to Mr. John Pendleton, that Miss Polly
was driven by Timothy to an early afternoon com-
mittee meeting of the Ladies' Aid Society. When
she returned at three o'clock, her cheeks were a
bright, pretty pink, and her hair, blown by the
damp wind, had fluffed into kinks and curls wherever the loosened pins had given leave.

Pollyanna had never before seen her aunt look
like this.

"Oh — oh — oh! Why, Aunt Polly, you've got
'em, too," she cried rapturously, dancing round and
round her aunt, as that lady entered the sitting
room.

"Got what, you impossible child?"

Pollyanna was still revolving round and round
her aunt.

"And I never knew you had 'em! *Can* folks
have 'em when you don't know they've got 'em?

162

Do you suppose I could?—'fore I get to Heaven, I mean," she cried, pulling out with eager fingers the straight locks above her ears. "But then, they wouldn't be black, if they did come. You can't hide the black part."

"Pollyanna, what does all this mean?" demanded Aunt Polly, hurriedly removing her hat, and trying to smooth back her disordered hair.

"No, no—please, Aunt Polly!" Pollyanna's jubilant voice turned to one of distressed appeal. "Don't smooth 'em out! It's those that I'm talking about—those darling little black curls. Oh, Aunt Polly, they're so pretty!"

"Nonsense! What do you mean, Pollyanna, by going to the Ladies' Aid the other day in that absurd fashion about that beggar boy?"

"But it isn't nonsense," urged Pollyanna, answering only the first of her aunt's remarks. "You don't know how pretty you look with your hair like that! Oh, Aunt Polly, please, mayn't I do your hair like I did Mrs. Snow's, and put in a flower? I'd so love to see you that way! Why, you'd be ever so much prettier than she was!"

"Pollyanna!" (Miss Polly spoke very sharply —all the more sharply because Pollyanna's words had given her an odd throb of joy: when before

had anybody cared how she, or her hair looked?
When before had anybody "loved" to see her
"pretty"?) "Pollyanna, you did not answer my
question. Why did you go to the Ladies' Aid in
that absurd fashion?"

"Yes'm, I know; but, please, I didn't know it
was absurd until I went and found out they'd rather
see their report grow than Jimmy. So then I wrote
to *my* Ladies' Aiders — 'cause Jimmy *is* far away
from them, you know; and I thought maybe he
could be their little India boy same as — Aunt
Polly, *was* I your little India girl? And, Aunt
Polly, you *will* let me do your hair, won't
you?"

Aunt Polly put her hand to her throat — the old,
helpless feeling was upon her, she knew.

"But, Pollyanna, when the ladies told me this
afternoon how you came to them, I was so
ashamed! I — "

Pollyanna began to dance up and down lightly
on her toes.

"You didn't! — you didn't say I *couldn't* do
your hair," she crowed triumphantly; "and so I'm
sure it means just the other way 'round, sort of —
like it did the other day about Mr. Pendleton's jelly
that you didn't send, but didn't want me to say you

didn't send, you know.   Now wait just where you
are.   I'll get a comb."

"But Pollyanna, Pollyanna," remonstrated Aunt
Polly, following the little girl from the room and
panting up-stairs after her.

"Oh, did you come up here?"   Pollyanna
greeted her at the door of Miss Polly's own room.
"That'll be nicer yet!   I've got the comb.   Now
sit down, please, right here.   Oh, I'm so glad you
let me do it!"

"But, Pollyanna, I — I — "

Miss Polly did not finish her sentence.   To her
helpless amazement she found herself in the low
chair before the dressing table, with her hair already tumbling about her ears under ten eager, but
very gentle fingers.

"Oh, my!   what pretty hair you've got," prattled
Pollyanna; "and there's so much more of it than
Mrs. Snow has, too!   But, of course, you need
more, anyhow, because you're well and can go to
places where folks can see it.   My!   I reckon folks'll
be glad when they do see it — and surprised, too,
'cause you've hid it so long.   Why, Aunt Polly, I'll
make you so pretty everybody'll just love to look
at you!"

"Pollyanna!" gasped a stifled but shocked voice

from a veil of hair. " I — I'm sure I don't know
why I'm letting you do this silly thing."

" Why, Aunt Polly, I should think you'd be glad
to have folks like to look at you! Don't you like
to look at pretty things? I'm ever so much happier
when I look at pretty folks, 'cause when I look at
the other kind I'm so sorry for them."

" But — but — "

" And I just love to do folks' hair," purred Pollyanna, contentedly. " I did quite a lot of the Ladies'
Aiders' — but there wasn't any of them so nice as
yours. Mrs. White's was pretty nice, though, and
she looked just lovely one day when I dressed her
up in — Oh, Aunt Polly, I've just happened to
think of something! But it's a secret, and I sha'n't
tell. Now your hair is almost done, and pretty
quick I'm going to leave you just a minute; and
you must promise — promise — *promise* not to stir
nor peek, even, till I come back. Now remember! "
she finished, as she ran from the room.

Aloud Miss Polly said nothing. To herself she
said that of course she should at once undo the
absurd work of her niece's fingers, and put her hair
up properly again. As for " peeking " — just as if
she cared how —

At that moment — unaccountably — Miss Polly

caught a glimpse of herself in the mirror of the
dressing table. And what she saw sent such a flush
of rosy color to her cheeks that — she only flushed
the more at the sight.

She saw a face — not young, it is true — but just
now alight with excitement and surprise. The
cheeks were a pretty pink. The eyes sparkled. The
hair, dark, and still damp from the outdoor air, lay
in loose waves about the forehead and curved back
over the ears in wonderfully becoming lines, with
softening little curls here and there.

So amazed and so absorbed was Miss Polly with
what she saw in the glass that she quite forgot her
determination to do over her hair, until she heard
Pollyanna enter the room again. Before she could
move, then, she felt a folded something slipped
across her eyes and tied in the back.

" Pollyanna, Pollyanna! What are you doing? "
she cried.

Pollyanna chuckled.

" That's just what I don't want you to know,
Aunt Polly, and I was afraid you *would* peek, so
I tied on the handkerchief. Now sit still. It won't
take but just a minute, then I'll let you see."

" But, Pollyanna," began Miss Polly, struggling
blindly to her feet, " you must take this off! **You**

— child, child! what *are* you doing?" she gasped, as she felt a soft something slipped about her shoulders.

Pollyanna only chuckled the more gleefully. With trembling fingers she was draping about her aunt's shoulders the fleecy folds of a beautiful lace shawl, yellowed from long years of packing away, and fragrant with lavender. Pollyanna had found the shawl the week before when Nancy had been regulating the attic; and it had occurred to her to-day that there was no reason why her aunt, as well as Mrs. White of her Western home, should not be " dressed up."

Her task completed, Pollyanna surveyed her work with eyes that approved, but that saw yet one touch wanting. Promptly, therefore, she pulled her aunt toward the sun parlor where she could see a belated red rose blooming on the trellis within reach of her hand.

" Pollyanna, what are you doing? Where are you taking me to?" recoiled Aunt Polly, vainly trying to hold herself back. " Pollyanna, I shall not — "

" It's just to the sun parlor — only a minute! I'll have you ready now quicker'n no time," panted Pollyanna, reaching for the rose and thrusting it

into the soft hair above Miss Polly's left ear.
"There!" she exulted, untying the knot of the
handkerchief and flinging the bit of linen far from
her. "Oh, Aunt Polly, now I reckon you'll be glad
I dressed you up!"

For one dazed moment Miss Polly looked at her
bedecked self, and at her surroundings; then she
gave a low cry and fled to her room. Pollyanna,
following the direction of her aunt's last dismayed
gaze, saw, through the open windows of the sun
parlor, the horse and gig turning into the driveway.
She recognized at once the man who held the reins.

Delightedly she leaned forward.

"Dr. Chilton, Dr. Chilton! Did you want to see
me? I'm up here."

"Yes," smiled the doctor, a little gravely. "Will
you come down, please?"

In the bedroom Pollyanna found a flushed-faced,
angry-eyed woman plucking at the pins that held
a lace shawl in place.

"Pollyanna, how could you?" moaned the
woman. "To think of your rigging me up like this,
and then letting me — *be seen!*"

Pollyanna stopped in dismay.

"But you looked lovely — perfectly lovely, Aunt
Polly; and — "

"'Lovely'!" scorned the woman, flinging the shawl to one side and attacking her hair with shaking fingers.

"Oh, Aunt Polly, please, please let the hair — stay!"

"Stay? Like this? As if I would!" And Miss Polly pulled the locks so tightly back that the last curl lay stretched dead at the ends of her fingers.

"O dear! And you did look so pretty," almost sobbed Pollyanna, as she stumbled through the door.

Down-stairs Pollyanna found the doctor waiting in his gig.

"I've prescribed you for a patient, and he's sent me to get the prescription filled," announced the doctor. "Will you go?"

"You mean — an errand — to the drug store?" asked Pollyanna, a little uncertainly. "I used to go some — for the Ladies' Aiders."

The doctor shook his head with a smile.

"Not exactly. It's Mr. John Pendleton. He would like to see you to-day, if you'll be so good as to come. It's stopped raining, so I drove down after you. Will you come? I'll call for you and bring you back before six o'clock."

"I'd love to!" exclaimed Pollyanna. "Let me ask Aunt Polly."

In a few moments she returned, hat in hand, but with rather a sober face.

"Didn't — your aunt want you to go?" asked the doctor, a little diffidently, as they drove away.

"Y-yes," sighed Pollyanna. "She — she wanted me to go *too* much, I'm afraid."

"Wanted you to go *too much!*"

Pollyanna sighed again.

"Yes. I reckon she meant she didn't want me there. You see, she said: 'Yes, yes, run along, run along — do! I wish you'd gone before.'"

The doctor smiled — but with his lips only. His eyes were very grave. For some time he said nothing; then, a little hesitatingly, he asked:

"Wasn't it — your aunt I saw with you a few minutes ago — in the window of the sun parlor?"

Pollyanna drew a long breath.

"Yes; that's what's the whole trouble, I suppose. You see I'd dressed her up in a perfectly lovely lace shawl I found up-stairs, and I'd fixed her hair and put on a rose, and she looked so pretty. Didn't *you* think she looked just lovely?"

For a moment the doctor did not answer. When he did speak his voice was so low Pollyanna could but just hear the words.

"Yes, Pollyanna, I — I thought she did look — just lovely."

"Did you? I'm so glad! I'll tell her," nodded the little girl, contentedly.

To her surprise the doctor gave a sudden exclamation.

"Never! Pollyanna, I — I'm afraid I shall have to ask you not to tell her — that."

"Why, Dr. Chilton! Why not? I should think you'd be glad —"

"But she might not be," cut in the doctor.

Pollyanna considered this for a moment.

"That's so — maybe she wouldn't," she sighed. "I remember now; 'twas 'cause she saw you that she ran. And she — she spoke afterwards about her being seen in that rig."

"I thought as much," declared the doctor, under his breath.

"Still, I don't see why," maintained Pollyanna, " — when she looked so pretty!"

The doctor said nothing. He did not speak again, indeed, until they were almost to the great stone house in which John Pendleton lay with a broken leg.

CHAPTER XVII

"JUST LIKE A BOOK"

JOHN PENDLETON greeted Pollyanna to-day with a smile.

"Well, Miss Pollyanna, I'm thinking you must be a very forgiving little person, else you wouldn't have come to see me again to-day."

"Why, Mr. Pendleton, I was real glad to come, and I'm sure I don't see why I shouldn't be, either."

"Oh, well, you know, I was pretty cross with you, I'm afraid, both the other day when you so kindly brought me the jelly, and that time when you found me with the broken leg at first. By the way, too, I don't think I've ever thanked you for that. Now I'm sure that even you would admit that you were very forgiving to come and see me, after such ungrateful treatment as that!"

Pollyanna stirred uneasily.

"But I was glad to find you — that is, I don't mean I was glad your leg was broken, of course," she corrected hurriedly.

John Pendleton smiled.

"I understand. Your tongue does get away with you once in a while, doesn't it, Miss Pollyanna? I do thank you, however; and I consider you a very brave little girl to do what you did that day. I thank you for the jelly, too," he added in a lighter voice.

"Did you like it?" asked Pollyanna with interest.

"Very much. I suppose — there isn't any more to-day that — that Aunt Polly *didn't* send, is there?" he asked with an odd smile.

His visitor looked distressed.

"N-no, sir." She hesitated, then went on with heightened color. "Please, Mr. Pendleton, I didn't mean to be rude the other day when I said Aunt Polly did *not* send the jelly."

There was no answer. John Pendleton was not smiling now. He was looking straight ahead of him with eyes that seemed to be gazing through and beyond the object before them. After a time he drew a long sigh and turned to Pollyanna. When he spoke his voice carried the old nervous fretfulness.

"Well, well, this will never do at all! I didn't send for you to see me moping this time. Listen! Out in the library — the big room where the tele-

phone is, you know — you will find a carved box
on the lower shelf of the big case with glass doors
in the corner not far from the fireplace. That is,
it'll be there if that confounded woman hasn't
' regulated ' it to somewhere else! You may bring
it to me. It is heavy, but not too heavy for you to
carry, I think."

" Oh, I'm awfully strong," declared Pollyanna,
cheerfully, as she sprang to her feet. In a minute
she had returned with the box.

It was a wonderful half-hour that Pollyanna
spent then. The box was full of treasures — curios
that John Pendleton had picked up in years of travel
— and concerning each there was some entertaining
story, whether it were a set of exquisitely carved
chessmen from China, or a little jade idol from
India.

It was after she had heard the story about the
idol that Pollyanna murmured wistfully:

" Well, I suppose it *would* be better to take a little
boy in India to bring up — one that didn't know
any more than to think that God was in that doll-
thing — than it would be to take Jimmy Bean, a
little boy who knows God is up in the sky. Still,
I can't help wishing they had wanted Jimmy Bean,
too, besides the India boys."

John Pendleton did not seem to hear. Again his eyes were staring straight before him, looking at nothing. But soon he had roused himself, and had picked up another curio to talk about.

The visit, certainly, was a delightful one, but before it was over, Pollyanna was realizing that they were talking about something besides the wonderful things in the beautiful carved box. They were talking of herself, of Nancy, of Aunt Polly, and of her daily life. They were talking, too, even of the life and home long ago in the far Western town.

Not until it was nearly time for her to go, did the man say, in a voice Pollyanna had never before heard from stern John Pendleton:

"Little girl, I want you to come to see me often. Will you? I'm lonesome, and I need you. There's another reason — and I'm going to tell you that, too. I thought, at first, after I found out who you were, the other day, that I didn't want you to come any more. You reminded me of — of something I have tried for long years to forget. So I said to myself that I never wanted to see you again; and every day, when the doctor asked if I wouldn't let him bring you to me, I said no.

"But after a time I found I was wanting to see

you so much that — that the fact that I *wasn't* seeing you was making me remember all the more
vividly the thing I was so wanting to forget. So
now I want you to come. Will you — little girl? "

" Why, yes, Mr. Pendleton," breathed Pollyanna,
her eyes luminous with sympathy for the sad-faced
man lying back on the pillow before her. " I'd love
to come! "

" Thank you," said John Pendleton, gently.

After supper that evening, Pollyanna, sitting on
the back porch, told Nancy all about Mr. John Pendleton's wonderful carved box, and the still more
wonderful things it contained.

" And ter think," sighed Nancy, " that he *showed*
ye all them things, and told ye about 'em like that
— him that's so cross he never talks ter no one —
no one! "

" Oh, but he isn't cross, Nancy, only outside,"
demurred Pollyanna, with quick loyalty. " I don't
see why everybody thinks he's so bad, either. They
wouldn't, if they knew him. But even Aunt Polly
doesn't like him very well. She wouldn't send the
jelly to him, you know, and she was so afraid he'd
think she did send it! "

" Probably she didn't call him no duty," shrugged

Nancy. "But what beats me is how he happened ter take ter you so, Miss Pollyanna — meanin' no offence ter you, of course — but he ain't the sort o' man what gen'rally takes ter kids; he ain't, he ain't."

Pollyanna smiled happily.

"But he did, Nancy," she nodded, "only I reckon even he didn't want to — *all* the time. Why, only to-day he owned up that one time he just felt he never wanted to see me again, because I reminded him of something he wanted to forget. But afterwards —"

"What's that?" interrupted Nancy, excitedly. "He said you reminded him of something he wanted to forget?"

"Yes. But afterwards —"

"What was it?" Nancy was eagerly insistent.

"He didn't tell me. He just said it was something."

"*The mystery!*" breathed Nancy, in an awestruck voice. "That's why he took to you in the first place. Oh, Miss Pollyanna! Why, that's just like a book — I've read lots of 'em; 'Lady Maud's Secret,' and 'The Lost Heir,' and 'Hidden for Years' — all of 'em had mysteries and things just like this. My stars and stockings! Just think of

havin' a book lived right under yer nose like this —
an' me not knowin' it all this time! Now tell me
everythin' — everythin' he said, Miss Pollyanna,
there's a dear! No wonder he took ter you; no
wonder — no wonder! "

"But he didn't," cried Pollyanna, "not till *I*
talked to *him,* first. And he didn't even know who
I was till I took the calf's-foot jelly, and had to
make him understand that Aunt Polly didn't send
it, and — "

Nancy sprang to her feet and clasped her hands
together suddenly.

"Oh, Miss Pollyanna, I know, I know — I *know*
I know!" she exulted rapturously. The next minute she was down at Pollyanna's side again. "Tell
me — now think, and answer straight and true,"
she urged excitedly. "It was after he found out
you was Miss Polly's niece that he said he didn't
ever want ter see ye again, wa'n't it?"

"Oh, yes. I told him that the last time I saw
him, and he told me this to-day."

"I thought as much," triumphed Nancy. "And
Miss Polly wouldn't send the jelly herself, would
she?"

"No."

"And you told him she didn't send it?"

" Why, yes; I — "

" And he began ter act queer and cry out sudden
after he found out you was her niece. He did that,
didn't he? "

" Why, y-yes; he did act a little queer — over
that jelly," admitted Pollyanna, with a thoughtful
frown.

Nancy drew a long sigh.

" Then I've got it, sure! Now listen. *Mr. John
Pendleton was Miss Polly Harrington's lover!* "
she announced impressively, but with a furtive
glance over her shoulder.

" Why, Nancy, he couldn't be! She doesn't like
him," objected Pollyanna.

Nancy gave her a scornful glance.

" Of course she don't! *That's* the quarrel! "

Pollyanna still looked incredulous, and with another long breath Nancy happily settled herself to
tell the story.

" It's like this. Just before you come, Mr. Tom
told me Miss Polly had had a lover once. I didn't
believe it. I couldn't — her and a lover! But Mr.
Tom said she had, and that he was livin' now right
in this town. And *now* I know, of course. It's
John Pendleton. Hain't he got a mystery in his
life? Don't he shut himself up in that grand house

alone, and never speak ter no one? Didn't he act
queer when he found out you was Miss Polly's
niece? And now hain't he owned up that you remind him of somethin' he wants ter forget? Just
as if *anybody* couldn't see 'twas Miss Polly! — an'
her sayin' she wouldn't send him no jelly, too.
Why, Miss Pollyanna, it's as plain as the nose on
yer face; it is, it is! "

"Oh-h! " breathed Pollyanna, in wide-eyed
amazement. " But, Nancy, I should think if they
loved each other they'd make up some time. Both
of 'em all alone, so, all these years. I should think
they'd be glad to make up! "

Nancy sniffed disdainfully.

" I guess maybe you don't know much about lovers, Miss Pollyanna. You ain't big enough yet,
anyhow. But if there *is* a set o' folks in the world
that wouldn't have no use for that 'ere ' glad game '
o' your'n, it'd be a pair o' quarrellin' lovers; and
that's what they be. Ain't he cross as sticks, most
gen'rally? — and ain't she — "

Nancy stopped abruptly, remembering just in
time to whom, and about whom, she was speaking.
Suddenly, however, she chuckled.

" I ain't sayin', though, Miss Pollyanna, but what
it would be a pretty slick piece of business if you

could *get* 'em ter playin' it — so they *would* be glad ter make up. But, my land! wouldn't folks stare some — Miss Polly and him! I guess, though, there ain't much chance, much chance!"

Pollyanna said nothing; but when she went into the house a little later, her face was very thought-ful.

CHAPTER XVIII

PRISMS

As the warm August days passed, Pollyanna went very frequently to the great house on Pendleton Hill. She did not feel, however, that her visits were really a success. Not but that the man seemed to want her there — he sent for her, indeed, frequently; but that when she was there, he seemed scarcely any the happier for her presence — at least, so Pollyanna thought.

He talked to her, it was true, and he showed her many strange and beautiful things — books, pictures, and curios. But he still fretted audibly over his own helplessness, and he chafed visibly under the rules and "regulatings" of the unwelcome members of his household. He did, indeed, seem to like to hear Pollyanna talk, however, and Pollyanna talked. Pollyanna liked to talk — but she was never sure that she would not look up and find him lying back on his pillow with that white, hurt look that always pained her; and she was never sure

183

which — if any — of her words had brought it there. As for telling him the " glad game," and trying to get him to play it — Pollyanna had never seen the time yet when she thought he would care to hear about it. She had twice tried to tell him; but neither time had she got beyond the beginning of what her father had said — John Pendleton had on each occasion turned the conversation abruptly to another subject.

Pollyanna never doubted now that John Pendleton was her Aunt Polly's one-time lover; and with all the strength of her loving, loyal heart, she wished she could in some way bring happiness into their — to her mind — miserably lonely lives.

Just how she was to do this, however, she could not see. She talked to Mr. Pendleton about her aunt; and he listened, sometimes politely, sometimes irritably, frequently with a quizzical smile on his usually stern lips. She talked to her aunt about Mr. Pendleton — or rather, she tried to talk to her about him. As a general thing, however, Miss Polly would not listen — long. She always found something else to talk about. She frequently did that, however, when Pollyanna was talking of others — of Dr. Chilton, for instance. Pollyanna laid this, though, to the fact that it had been Dr.

Chilton who had seen her in the sun parlor with the rose in her hair and the lace shawl draped about her shoulders. Aunt Polly, indeed, seemed particularly bitter against Dr. Chilton, as Pollyanna found out one day when a hard cold shut her up in the house.

"If you are not better by night I shall send for the doctor," Aunt Polly said.

"Shall you? Then I'm going to be worse," gurgled Pollyanna. "I'd love to have Dr. Chilton come to see me!"

She wondered, then, at the look that came to her aunt's face.

"It will not be Dr. Chilton, Pollyanna," Miss Polly said sternly. "Dr. Chilton is not our family physician. I shall send for Dr. Warren — if you are worse."

Pollyanna did not grow worse, however, and Dr. Warren was not summoned.

"And I'm so glad, too," Pollyanna said to her aunt that evening. "Of course I like Dr. Warren, and all that; but I like Dr. Chilton better, and I'm afraid he'd feel hurt if I didn't have him. You see, he wasn't really to blame, after all, that he happened to see you when I'd dressed you up so pretty that day, Aunt Polly," she finished wistfully.

" That will do, Pollyanna. I really do not wish
to discuss Dr. Chilton — or his feelings," reproved
Miss Polly, decisively.

Pollyanna looked at her for a moment with
mournfully interested eyes; then she sighed:

" I just love to see you when your cheeks are
pink like that, Aunt Polly; but I would so like to
fix your hair. If —   Why, Aunt Polly! " But
her aunt was already out of sight down the
hall.

It was toward the end of August that Pollyanna,
making an early morning call on John Pendleton,
found the flaming band of blue and gold and green
edged with red and violet lying across his pillow.
She stopped short in awed delight.

" Why, Mr. Pendleton, it's a baby rainbow — a
real rainbow come in to pay you a visit! " she exclaimed, clapping her hands together softly. " Oh
— oh — oh, how pretty it is! But how *did* it get
in? " she cried.

The man laughed a little grimly: John Pendleton was particularly out of sorts with the world this
morning.

" Well, I suppose it ' got in ' through the bevelled
edge of that glass thermometer in the window," he

said wearily. " The sun shouldn't strike it at all —
but it does in the morning."

" Oh, but it's so pretty, Mr. Pendleton! And
does just the sun do that? My! if it was mine I'd
have it hang in the sun all day long!"

" Lots of good you'd get out of the thermometer,
then," laughed the man. " How do you suppose
you could tell how hot it was, or how cold it was,
if the thermometer hung in the sun all day?"

" I shouldn't care," breathed Pollyanna, her fas-
cinated eyes on the brilliant band of colors across
the pillow. " Just as if anybody'd care — when
they were living all the time in a rainbow!"

The man laughed. He was watching Pollyanna's rapt face a little curiously. Suddenly a new
thought came to him. He touched the bell at his
side.

" Nora," he said, when the elderly maid appeared
at the door, " bring me one of the big brass candle-
sticks from the mantel in the front drawing-room."

" Yes, sir," murmured the woman, looking
slightly dazed. In a minute she had returned. A
musical tinkling entered the room with her as she
advanced wonderingly toward the bed. It came
from the prism pendants encircling the old-fash-
ioned candelabrum in her hand.

" Thank you. You may set it here on the stand,"
directed the man. " Now get a string and fasten
it to the sash-curtain fixtures of that window
there. Take down the sash-curtain, and let the
string reach straight across the window from
side to side. That will be all. Thank you,"
he said, when she had carried out his directions.

As she left the room he turned smiling eyes
toward the wondering Pollyanna.

" Bring me the candlestick now, please, Pollyanna."

With both hands she brought it; and in a moment he was slipping off the pendants, one by one,
until they lay, a round dozen of them, side by side,
on the bed.

" Now, my dear, suppose you take them and
hook them to that little string Nora fixed across the
window. If you really *want* to live in a rainbow —
I don't see but we'll have to have a rainbow for you
to live in! "

Pollyanna had not hung up three of the pendants
in the sunlit window before she saw a little of what
was going to happen. She was so excited then she
could scarcely control her shaking fingers enough
to hang up the rest. But at last her task was fin-

ished, and she stepped back with a low cry of delight.

It had become a fairyland — that sumptuous, but dreary bedroom. Everywhere were bits of dancing red and green, violet and orange, gold and blue. The wall, the floor, and the furniture, even to the bed itself, were aflame with shimmering bits of color.

"Oh, oh, oh, how lovely!" breathed Pollyanna; then she laughed suddenly. "I just reckon the sun himself is trying to play the game now, don't you?" she cried, forgetting for the moment that Mr. Pendleton could not know what she was talking about. "Oh, how I wish I had a lot of those things! How I would like to give them to Aunt Polly and Mrs. Snow and — lots of folks. I reckon *then* they'd be glad all right! Why, I think even Aunt Polly'd get so glad she couldn't help banging doors — if she lived in a rainbow like that. Don't you?"

Mr. Pendleton laughed.

"Well, from my remembrance of your aunt, Miss Pollyanna, I must say I think it would take something more than a few prisms in the sunlight to — to make her bang many doors — for gladness. But come, now, really, what do you mean?"

Pollyanna stared slightly; then she drew a long breath.

"Oh, I forgot. You don't know about the game. I remember now."

"Suppose you tell me, then."

And this time Pollyanna told him. She told him the whole thing from the very first — from the crutches that should have been a doll. As she talked, she did not look at his face. Her rapt eyes were still on the dancing flecks of color from the prism pendants swaying in the sunlit window.

"And that's all," she sighed, when she had finished. "And now you know why I said the sun was trying to play it — that game."

For a moment there was silence. Then a low voice from the bed said unsteadily:

"Perhaps; but I'm thinking that the very finest prism of them all is yourself, Pollyanna."

"Oh, but I don't show beautiful red and green and purple when the sun shines through me, Mr. Pendleton!"

"Don't you?" smiled the man. And Pollyanna, looking into his face, wondered why there were tears in his eyes.

"No," she said. Then, after a minute she added mournfully: "I'm afraid, Mr. Pendleton, the sun

doesn't make anything but freckles — out of me.
Aunt Polly says it *does* make them!"

The man laughed a little; and again Pollyanna
looked at him: the laugh had sounded almost like
a sob.

CHAPTER XIX

WHICH IS SOMEWHAT SURPRISING

POLLYANNA entered school in September. Preliminary examinations showed that she was well advanced for a girl of her years, and she was soon a happy member of a class of girls and boys her own age.

School, in some ways, was a surprise to Pollyanna; and Pollyanna, certainly, in many ways, was very much of a surprise to school. They were soon on the best of terms, however, and to her aunt Pollyanna confessed that going to school *was* living, after all — though she had had her doubts before.

In spite of her delight in her new work, Pollyanna did not forget her old friends. True, she could not give them quite so much time now, of course; but she gave them what time she could. Perhaps John Pendleton, of them all, however, was the most dissatisfied.

One Saturday afternoon he spoke to her about it.

"See here, Pollyanna, how would you like to come and live with me?" he asked, a little impatiently. "I don't see anything of you, nowadays."

Pollyanna laughed — Mr. Pendleton was such a funny man!

"I thought you didn't like to have folks 'round," she said.

He made a wry face.

"Oh, but that was before you taught me to play that wonderful game of yours. *Now* I'm glad to be waited on, hand and foot! Never mind, I'll be on my own two feet yet, one of these days; then I'll see who steps around," he finished, picking up one of the crutches at his side and shaking it playfully at the little girl. They were sitting in the great library to-day.

"Oh, but you aren't really glad at all for things; you just *say* you are," pouted Pollyanna, her eyes on the dog, dozing before the fire. "You know you don't play the game right *ever*, Mr. Pendleton — you know you don't!"

The man's face grew suddenly very grave.

"That's why I want you, little girl — to help me play it. Will you come?"

Pollyanna turned in surprise.

" Mr. Pendleton, you don't really mean — that? "

" But I do. I want you. Will you come? "

Pollyanna looked distressed.

" Why, Mr. Pendleton, I can't — you know I can't. Why, I'm — Aunt Polly's! "

A quick something crossed the man's face that Pollyanna could not quite understand. His head came up almost fiercely.

" You're no more hers than — Perhaps she would let you come to me," he finished more gently. " Would you come — if she did? "

Pollyanna frowned in deep thought.

" But Aunt Polly has been so — good to me," she began slowly; " and she took me when I didn't have anybody left but the Ladies' Aid, and — "

Again that spasm of something crossed the man's face; but this time, when he spoke, his voice was low and very sad.

" Pollyanna, long years ago I loved somebody very much. I hoped to bring her, some day, to this house. I pictured how happy we'd be together in our home all the long years to come."

" Yes," pitied Pollyanna, her eyes shining with sympathy.

" But — well, I didn't bring her here. Never

mind why. I just didn't — that's all. And ever since then this great gray pile of stone has been a house — never a home. It takes a woman's hand and heart, or a child's presence, to make a home, Pollyanna; and I have not had either. Now will you come, my dear?"

Pollyanna sprang to her feet. Her face was fairly illumined.

"Mr. Pendleton, you — you mean that you wish you — you had had that woman's hand and heart all this time?"

"Why, y-yes, Pollyanna."

"Oh, I'm so glad! Then it's all right," sighed the little girl. "Now you can take us both, and everything will be lovely."

"Take — you — both?" repeated the man, dazedly.

A faint doubt crossed Pollyanna's countenance.

"Well, of course, Aunt Polly isn't won over, yet; but I'm sure she will be if you tell it to her just as you did to me, and then we'd both come, of course."

A look of actual terror leaped to the man's eyes.

"Aunt Polly come — *here!*"

Pollyanna's eyes widened a little.

"Would you rather go *there?*" she asked. "Of

course the house isn't quite so pretty, but it's nearer — "

" Pollyanna, what *are* you talking about? " asked the man, very gently now.

" Why, about where we're going to live, of course," rejoined Pollyanna, in obvious surprise. " I *thought* you meant here, at first. You said it was here that you had wanted Aunt Polly's hand and heart all these years to make a home, and — "

An inarticulate cry came from the man's throat. He raised his hand and began to speak; but the next moment he dropped his hand nervelessly at his side.

" The doctor, sir," said the maid in the doorway.

Pollyanna rose at once.

John Pendleton turned to her feverishly.

" Pollyanna, for Heaven's sake, say nothing of what I asked you — yet," he begged, in a low voice.

Pollyanna dimpled into a sunny smile.

" Of course not! Just as if I didn't know you'd rather tell her yourself!" she called back merrily over her shoulder.

John Pendleton fell limply back in his chair.

" Why, what's up? " demanded the doctor, a minute later, his fingers on his patient's galloping pulse.

A whimsical smile trembled on John Pendleton's lips.

" Overdose of your — tonic, I guess," he laughed, as he noted the doctor's eyes following Pollyanna's little figure down the driveway.

CHAPTER XX

WHICH IS MORE SURPRISING

SUNDAY mornings Pollyanna usually attended church and Sunday school. Sunday afternoons she frequently went for a walk with Nancy. She had planned one for the day after her Saturday afternoon visit to Mr. John Pendleton; but on the way home from Sunday school Dr. Chilton overtook her in his gig, and brought his horse to a stop.

"Suppose you let me drive you home, Pollyanna," he suggested. "I want to speak to you a minute. I was just driving out to your place to tell you," he went on, as Pollyanna settled herself at his side. "Mr. Pendleton sent a special request for you to go to see him this afternoon, *sure*. He says it's very important."

Pollyanna nodded happily.

"Yes, it is, I know. I'll go."

The doctor eyed her with some surprise.

"I'm not sure I shall let you, after all," he declared, his eyes twinkling. "You seemed more upsetting than soothing yesterday, young lady."

Pollyanna laughed.

" Oh, it wasn't me, truly — not really, you know ; not so much as it was Aunt Polly."

The doctor turned with a quick start.

" Your — aunt ! " he ejaculated.

Pollyanna gave a happy little bounce in her seat.

" Yes. And it's so exciting and lovely, just like a story, you know. I — I'm going to tell you," she burst out, with sudden decision. " He said not to mention it ; but he wouldn't mind your knowing, of course. He meant not to mention it to *her*."

" *Her?* "

" Yes ; Aunt Polly. And, of course he *would* want to tell her himself instead of having me do it — lovers, so ! "

" Lovers ! " As the doctor said the word, the horse started violently, as if the hand that held the reins had given them a sharp jerk.

" Yes," nodded Pollyanna, happily. " That's the story-part, you see. I didn't know it till Nancy told me. She said Aunt Polly had a lover years ago. and they quarrelled. She didn't know who it was at first. But we've found out now. It's Mr. Pendleton, you know."

The doctor relaxed suddenly. The hand holding the reins fell limply to his lap.

"Oh! No; I — didn't know," he said quietly.

Pollyanna hurried on — they were nearing the Harrington homestead.

"Yes; and I'm so glad now. It's come out lovely. Mr. Pendleton asked me to come and live with him, but of course I wouldn't leave Aunt Polly like that — after she'd been so good to me. Then he told me all about the woman's hand and heart that he used to want, and I found out that he wanted it now; and I was so glad! For of course if he *wants* to make up the quarrel, everything will be all right now, and Aunt Polly and I will both go to live there, or else he'll come to live with us. Of course Aunt Polly doesn't know yet, and we haven't got everything settled; so I suppose that is why he wanted to see me this afternoon, sure."

The doctor sat suddenly erect. There was an odd smile on his lips.

"Yes; I can well imagine that Mr. John Pendleton does — want to see you, Pollyanna," he nodded, as he pulled his horse to a stop before the door.

"There's Aunt Polly now in the window," cried Pollyanna; then, a second later: "Why, no, she isn't — but I thought I saw her!"

"No; she isn't there — now," said the doctor. His lips had suddenly lost their smile.

Pollyanna found a very nervous John Pendleton waiting for her that afternoon.

"Pollyanna," he began at once. "I've been trying all night to puzzle out what you meant by all that, yesterday — about my wanting your Aunt Polly's hand and heart here all those years. What did you mean?"

"Why, because you were lovers, you know — once; and I was so glad you still felt that way now."

"Lovers! — your Aunt Polly and I?"

At the obvious surprise in the man's voice, Pollyanna opened wide her eyes.

"Why, Mr. Pendleton, Nancy said you were!"

The man gave a short little laugh.

"Indeed! Well, I'm afraid I shall have to say that Nancy — didn't know."

"Then you — weren't lovers?" Pollyanna's voice was tragic with dismay.

"Never!"

"And it *isn't* all coming out like a book?"

There was no answer. The man's eyes were moodily fixed out the window.

"O dear! And it was all going so splendidly," almost sobbed Pollyanna. "I'd have been so glad to come — with Aunt Polly."

"And you won't — now?" The man asked the question without turning his head.

"Of course not! I'm Aunt Polly's."

The man turned now, almost fiercely.

"Before you were hers, Pollyanna, you were — your mother's. And — it was your mother's hand and heart that I wanted long years ago."

"My mother's!"

"Yes. I had not meant to tell you, but perhaps it's better, after all, that I do — now." John Pendleton's face had grown very white. He was speaking with evident difficulty. Pollyanna, her eyes wide and frightened, and her lips parted, was gazing at him fixedly. "I loved your mother; but she — didn't love me. And after a time she went away with — your father. I did not know until then how much I did — care. The whole world suddenly seemed to turn black under my fingers, and — But, never mind. For long years I have been a cross, crabbed, unlovable, unloved old man — though I'm not nearly sixty, yet, Pollyanna. Then, one day, like one of the prisms that you love so well, little girl, you danced into my life, and flecked my dreary old world with dashes of the purple and gold and scarlet of your own bright cheeriness. I found out, after a time, who you

were, and — and I thought then I never wanted
to see you again. I didn't want to be reminded
of — your mother. But — you know how that
came out. I just had to have you come. And now
I want you always. Pollyanna, won't you come —
now?"

"But, Mr. Pendleton, I — There's Aunt
Polly!" Pollyanna's eyes were blurred with tears.

The man made an impatient gesture.

"What about me? How do you suppose I'm
going to be 'glad' about anything — without you?
Why, Pollyanna, it's only since you came that I've
been even half glad to live! But if I had you for
my own little girl, I'd be glad for — anything;
and I'd try to make you glad, too, my dear. You
shouldn't have a wish ungratified. All my money,
to the last cent, should go to make you happy."

Pollyanna looked shocked.

"Why, Mr. Pendleton, as if I'd let you spend
it on me — all that money you've saved for the
heathen!"

A dull red came to the man's face. He started
to speak, but Pollyanna was still talking.

"Besides, anybody with such a lot of money as
you have doesn't need me to make you glad about
things. You're making other folks so glad giving

them things that you just can't help being glad
yourself! Why, look at those prisms you gave Mrs.
Snow and me, and the gold piece you gave Nancy
on her birthday, and —"

"Yes, yes — never mind about all that," interrupted the man. His face was very, very red now
— and no wonder, perhaps: it was not for " giving things " that John Pendleton had been best
known in the past. " That's all nonsense. 'Twasn't
much, anyhow — but what there was, was because
of you. *You* gave those things; not I! Yes, you
did," he repeated, in answer to the shocked denial
in her face. " And that only goes to prove all the
more how I need you, little girl," he added, his
voice softening into tender pleading once more.
" If ever, ever I am to play the ' glad game,' Pollyanna, you'll have to come and play it with me."

The little girl's forehead puckered into a wistful
frown.

" Aunt Polly has been so good to me," she began;
but the man interrupted her sharply. The old irri-
tability had come back to his face. Impatience
which would brook no opposition had been a part
of John Pendleton's nature too long to yield very
easily now to restraint.

" Of course she's been good to you! But she

doesn't want you, I'll warrant, half so much as I do," he contested.

"Why, Mr. Pendleton, she's glad, I know, to have — "

"Glad!" interrupted the man, thoroughly losing his patience now. "I'll wager Miss Polly doesn't know how to be glad — for anything! Oh, she does her duty, I know. She's a very *dutiful* woman. I've had experience with her 'duty,' before. I'll acknowledge we haven't been the best of friends for the last fifteen or twenty years. But I know her. Every one knows her — and she isn't the 'glad' kind, Pollyanna. She doesn't know how to be. As for your coming to me — you just ask her and see if she won't let you come. And, oh, little girl, little girl, I want you so!" he finished brokenly.

Pollyanna rose to her feet with a long sigh.

"All right. I'll ask her," she said wistfully. "Of course I don't mean that I wouldn't like to live here with you, Mr. Pendleton, but — " She did not complete her sentence. There was a moment's silence, then she added: "Well, anyhow, I'm glad I didn't tell her yesterday; — 'cause then I supposed *she* was wanted, too."

John Pendleton smiled grimly.

" Well, yes, Pollyanna; I guess it is just as well you didn't mention it — yesterday."

" I didn't — only to the doctor; and of course he doesn't count."

" The doctor!" cried John Pendleton, turning quickly. " Not — Dr. — Chilton?"

" Yes; when he came to tell me you wanted to see me to-day, you know."

" Well, of all the — " muttered the man, falling back in his chair. Then he sat up with sudden interest. " And what did Dr. Chilton say?" he asked.

Pollyanna frowned thoughtfully.

" Why, I don't remember. Not much, I reckon. Oh, he did say he could well imagine you did want to see me."

" Oh, did he, indeed!" answered John Pendleton. And Pollyanna wondered why he gave that sudden queer little laugh.

CHAPTER XXI

A QUESTION ANSWERED

THE sky was darkening fast with what appeared to be an approaching thunder shower when Polly-anna hurried down the hill from John Pendleton's house. Half-way home she met Nancy with an umbrella. By that time, however, the clouds had shifted their position and the shower was not so imminent.

"Guess it's goin' 'round ter the north," announced Nancy, eyeing the sky critically. "I thought 'twas, all the time, but Miss Polly wanted me ter come with this. She was *worried* about ye!"

"Was she?" murmured Pollyanna abstractedly, eyeing the clouds in her turn.

Nancy sniffed a little.

"You don't seem ter notice what I said," she observed aggrievedly. "I said yer aunt was *worried* about ye!"

"Oh," sighed Pollyaana, remembering suddenly

207

the question she was so soon to ask her aunt. " I'm sorry. I didn't mean to scare her."

" Well, I'm glad," retorted Nancy, unexpectedly. " I am, I am."

Pollyanna stared.

" *Glad* that Aunt Polly was scared about me! Why, Nancy, *that* isn't the way to play the game — to be glad for things like that!" she objected.

" There wa'n't no game in it," retorted Nancy. " Never thought of it. *You* don't seem ter sense what it means ter have Miss Polly *worried* about ye, child!"

" Why, it means worried — and worried is horrid — to feel," maintained Pollyanna. " What else can it mean?"

Nancy tossed her head.

" Well, I'll tell ye what it means. It means she's at last gettin' down somewheres near human — like folks; an' that she ain't jest doin' her duty by ye all the time."

" Why, Nancy," demurred the scandalized Pollyanna, " Aunt Polly always does her duty. She — she's a very dutiful woman!" Unconsciously Pollyanna repeated John Pendleton's words of half an hour before.

Nancy chuckled.

"You're right she is — and she always was, I
guess! But she's somethin' more, now, since you
came."

Pollyanna's face changed. Her brows drew into
a troubled frown.

"There, that's what I was going to ask you,
Nancy," she sighed. "Do you think Aunt Polly
likes to have me here? Would she mind — if —
if I wasn't here any more?"

Nancy threw a quick look into the little girl's
absorbed face. She had expected to be asked this
question long before, and she had dreaded it. She
had wondered how she should answer it — how
she could answer it honestly without cruelly hurting
the questioner. But now, *now*, in the face of the
new suspicions that had become convictions by the
afternoon's umbrella-sending — Nancy only welcomed the question with open arms. She was sure
that, with a clean conscience to-day, she could set
the love-hungry little girl's heart at rest.

"Likes ter have ye here? Would she miss ye
if ye wa'n't here?" cried Nancy, indignantly. "As
if that wa'n't jest what I was tellin' of ye! Didn't
she send me posthaste with an umbrella 'cause she
see a little cloud in the sky? Didn't she make me
tote yer things all down-stairs, so you could have

the pretty room you wanted? Why, Miss Pollyanna, when ye remember how at first she hated ter
have — ”

With a choking cough Nancy pulled herself up
just in time.

“ And it ain’t jest things I can put my fingers
on, neither,” rushed on Nancy, breathlessly. “ It’s
little ways she has, that shows how you’ve been
softenin’ her up an’ mellerin’ her down — the cat,
and the dog, and the way she speaks ter me, and —
oh, lots o’ things. Why, Miss Pollyanna, there
ain’t no tellin’ how she’d miss ye — if ye wa’n’t
here,” finished Nancy, speaking with an enthusiastic
certainty that was meant to hide the perilous admis-
sion she had almost made before. Even then she
was not quite prepared for the sudden joy that
illumined Pollyanna’s face.

“ Oh, Nancy, I’m so glad — glad — glad! You
don’t know how glad I am that Aunt Polly — wants
me! ”

“ As if I’d leave her now! ” thought Pollyanna,
as she climbed the stairs to her room a little later.
“ I always knew I wanted to live with Aunt Polly
— but I reckon maybe I didn’t know quite how
much I wanted Aunt Polly — to want to live with
me! ”

The task of telling John Pendleton of her decision would not be an easy one, Pollyanna knew, and she dreaded it. She was very fond of John Pendleton, and she was very sorry for him — because he seemed to be so sorry for himself. She was sorry, too, for the long, lonely life that had made him so unhappy; and she was grieved that it had been because of her mother that he had spent those dreary years. She pictured the great gray house as it would be after its master was well again, with its silent rooms, its littered floors, its disordered desk; and her heart ached for his loneliness. She wished that somewhere, some one might be found who— And it was at this point that she sprang to her feet with a little cry of joy at the thought that had come to her.

As soon as she could, after that, she hurried up the hill to John Pendleton's house; and in due time she found herself in the great dim library, with John Pendleton himself sitting near her, his long, thin hands lying idle on the arms of his chair, and his faithful little dog at his feet.

"Well, Pollyanna, is it to be the 'glad game' with me, all the rest of my life?" asked the man, gently.

"Oh, yes," cried Pollyanna. "I've thought of

the very gladdest kind of a thing for you to do, and — "

" With — *you?* " asked John Pendleton, his mouth growing a little stern at the corners.

" N-no; but — "

" Pollyanna, you aren't going to say no! " interrupted a voice deep with emotion.

" I — I've got to, Mr. Pendleton; truly I have. Aunt Polly — "

" Did she *refuse* — to let you — come? "

" I — I didn't ask her," stammered the little girl, miserably.

" Pollyanna! "

Pollyanna turned away her eyes. She could not meet the hurt, grieved gaze of her friend.

" So you didn't even ask her! "

" I couldn't, sir — truly," faltered Pollyanna. " You see, I found out — without asking. Aunt Polly *wants* me with her, and — and I want to stay, too," she confessed bravely. " You don't know how good she's been to me; and — and I think, really, sometimes she's beginning to be glad about things — lots of things. And you know she never used to be. You said it yourself. Oh, Mr. Pendleton, I *couldn't* leave Aunt Polly — now! "

There was a long pause. Only the snapping of

the wood fire in the grate broke the silence. At last, however, the man spoke.

" No, Pollyanna; I see. You couldn't leave her — now," he said. " I won't ask you — again." The last word was so low it was almost inaudible; but Pollyanna heard.

" Oh, but you don't know about the rest of it," she reminded him eagerly. "There's the very gladdest thing you *can* do — truly there is ! "

" Not for me, Pollyanna."

" Yes, sir, for you. You *said* it. You said only a — a woman's hand and heart or a child's presence could make a home. And I can get it for you — a child's presence; — not me, you know, but another one."

" As if I would have any but you ! " resented an indignant voice.

" But you will — when you know; you're so kind and good! Why, think of the prisms and the gold pieces, and all that money you save for the heathen, and — "

" Pollyanna ! " interrupted the man, savagely. " Once for all let us end that nonsense! I've tried to tell you half a dozen times before. There *is* no money for the heathen. I never sent a penny to them in my life. There ! "

He lifted his chin and braced himself to meet what he expected — the grieved disappointment of Pollyanna's eyes. To his amazement, however, there was neither grief nor disappointment in Pollyanna's eyes. There was only surprised joy.

" Oh, oh! " she cried, clapping her hands. " I'm so glad! That is," she corrected, coloring distressfully, " I don't mean that I'm not sorry for the heathen, only just now I can't help being glad that you don't want the little India boys, because all the rest have wanted them. And so I'm glad you'd rather have Jimmy Bean. Now I know you'll take him! "

" Take — *who?* "

" Jimmy Bean. He's the ' child's presence,' you know; and he'll be so glad to be it. I had to tell him last week that even my Ladies' Aid out West wouldn't take him, and he was so disappointed. But now — when he hears of this — he'll be so glad! "

" Will he? Well, I won't," ejaculated the man, decisively. " Pollyanna, this is sheer nonsense! "

" You don't mean — you won't take him? "

" I certainly do mean just that."

" But he'd be a lovely child's presence," faltered

Pollyanna. She was almost crying now. "And you *couldn't* be lonesome — with Jimmy 'round."

"I don't doubt it," rejoined the man; "but — I think I prefer the lonesomeness."

It was then that Pollyanna, for the first time in weeks, suddenly remembered something Nancy had once told her. She raised her chin aggrievedly.

"Maybe you think a nice live little boy wouldn't be better than that old dead skeleton you keep somewhere; but I think it would!"

"*Skeleton?*"

"Yes. Nancy said you had one in your closet, somewhere."

"Why, what — " Suddenly the man threw back his head and laughed. He laughed very heartily indeed — so heartily that Pollyanna began to cry from pure nervousness. When he saw that, John Pendleton sat erect very promptly. His face grew grave at once.

"Pollyanna, I suspect you are right — more right than you know," he said gently. "In fact, I *know* that a 'nice live little boy' would be far better than — my skeleton in the closet; only — we aren't always willing to make the exchange. We are apt to still cling to — our skeletons, Pollyanna. However, suppose you tell me a little more about this nice little boy." And Pollyanna told him.

Perhaps the laugh cleared the air; or perhaps the pathos of Jimmy Bean's story as told by Pollyanna's eager little lips touched a heart already strangely softened. At all events, when Pollyanna went home that night she carried with her an invitation for Jimmy Bean himself to call at the great house with Pollyanna the next Saturday afternoon.

"And I'm so glad, and I'm sure you'll like him," sighed Pollyanna, as she said good-by. "I do so want Jimmy Bean to have a home — and folks that care, you know."

CHAPTER XXII

SERMONS AND WOODBOXES

On the afternoon that Pollyanna told John Pendleton of Jimmy Bean, the Rev. Paul Ford climbed
the hill and entered the Pendleton Woods, hoping
that the hushed beauty of God's out-of-doors would
still the tumult that His children of men had
wrought.

The Rev. Paul Ford was sick at heart. Month
by month, for a year past, conditions in the parish
under him had been growing worse and worse;
until it seemed that now, turn which way he would,
he encountered only wrangling, backbiting, scandal,
and jealousy. He had argued, pleaded, rebuked,
and ignored by turns; and always and through all
he had prayed — earnestly, hopefully. But to-day
miserably he was forced to own that matters were
no better, but rather worse.

Two of his deacons were at swords' points over
a silly something that only endless brooding had
made of any account. Three of his most energetic

women workers had withdrawn from the Ladies'
Aid Society because a tiny spark of gossip had been
fanned by wagging tongues into a devouring flame
of scandal. The choir had split over the amount of
solo work given to a fanciedly preferred singer.
Even the Christian Endeavor Society was in a
ferment of unrest owing to open criticism of two
of its officers. As to the Sunday school — it had
been the resignation of its superintendent and two
of its teachers that had been the last straw, and
that had sent the harassed minister to the quiet
woods for prayer and meditation.

Under the green arch of the trees the Rev. Paul
Ford faced the thing squarely. To his mind, the
crisis had come. Something must be done — and
done at once. The entire work of the church was
at a standstill. The Sunday services, the week-day
prayer meeting, the missionary teas, even the suppers and socials were becoming less and less well
attended. True, a few conscientious workers were
still left. But they pulled at cross purposes, usually;
and always they showed themselves to be acutely
aware of the critical eyes all about them, and of
the tongues that had nothing to do but to talk about
what the eyes saw.

And because of all this, the Rev. Paul Ford

understood very well that he (God's minister), the church, the town, and even Christianity itself was suffering; and must suffer still more unless —

Clearly something must be done, and done at once. But what?

Slowly the minister took from his pocket the notes he had made for his next Sunday's sermon. Frowningly he looked at them. His mouth settled into stern lines, as aloud, very impressively, he read the verses on which he had determined to speak:

" ' But woe unto you, scribes and Pharisees, hypocrites! for ye shut up the kingdom of heaven against men: for ye neither go in yourselves, neither suffer ye them that are entering to go in.'

" ' Woe unto you, scribes and Pharisees, hypocrites! for ye devour widows' houses, and for a pretence make long prayer: therefore ye shall receive the greater damnation.'

" ' Woe unto you, scribes and Pharisees, hypocrites! for ye pay tithe of mint and anise and cummin, and have omitted the weightier matters of the law, judgment, mercy, and faith: these ought ye to have done, and not to leave the other undone.' "

It was a bitter denunciation. In the green aisles of the woods, the minister's deep voice rang out with scathing effect. Even the birds and squirrels seemed hushed into awed silence. It brought to the minister a vivid realization of how those words would sound the next Sunday when he should utter them before his people in the sacred hush of the church.

His people! — they *were* his people. Could he do it? Dare he do it? Dare he *not* do it? It was a fearful denunciation, even without the words that would follow — his own words. He had prayed and prayed. He had pleaded earnestly for help, for guidance. He longed — oh, how earnestly he longed! — to take now, in this crisis, the right step. But was this — the right step?

Slowly the minister folded the papers and thrust them back into his pocket. Then, with a sigh that was almost a moan, he flung himself down at the foot of a tree, and covered his face with his hands.

It was there that Pollyanna, on her way home from the Pendleton house, found him. With a little cry she ran forward.

"Oh, oh, Mr. Ford! You — *you* haven't broken *your* leg or — or anything, have you?" she gasped.

The minister dropped his hands, and looked up quickly. He tried to smile.

"No, dear — no, indeed! I'm just — resting."

"Oh," sighed Pollyanna, falling back a little. "That's all right, then. You see, Mr. Pendleton *had* broken his leg when I found him — but he was lying down, though. And you are sitting up."

"Yes, I am sitting up; and I haven't broken anything — that doctors can mend."

The last words were very low, but Pollyanna heard them. A swift change crossed her face. Her eyes glowed with tender sympathy.

"I know what you mean — something plagues you. Father used to feel like that, lots of times. I reckon ministers do — most generally. You see there's such a lot depends on 'em, somehow."

The Rev. Paul Ford turned a little wonderingly.

"Was *your* father a minister, Pollyanna?"

"Yes, sir. Didn't you know? I supposed everybody knew that. He married Aunt Polly's sister, and she was my mother."

"Oh, I understand. But, you see, I haven't been here many years, so I don't know all the family histories."

"Yes, sir — I mean, no, sir," smiled Pollyanna.

There was a long pause. The minister, still sitting at the foot of the tree, appeared to have forgotten Pollyanna's presence. He had pulled some papers from his pocket and unfolded them; but he was not looking at them. He was gazing, instead, at a leaf on the ground a little distance away — and it was not even a pretty leaf. It was brown and dead. Pollyanna, looking at him, felt vaguely sorry for him.

"It — it's a nice day," she began hopefully.

For a moment there was no answer; then the minister looked up with a start.

"What? Oh! — yes, it is a very nice day."

"And 'tisn't cold at all, either, even if 'tis October," observed Pollyanna, still more hopefully. "Mr. Pendleton had a fire, but he said he didn't need it. It was just to look at. I like to look at fires, don't you?"

There was no reply this time, though Pollyanna waited patiently, before she tried again — by a new route.

"Do you like being a minister?"

The Rev. Paul Ford looked up now, very quickly.

"Do I like — Why, what an odd question! Why do you ask that, my dear?"

"Nothing — only the way you looked. It made me think of my father. He used to look like that — sometimes."

"Did he?" The minister's voice was polite, but

his eyes had gone back to the dried leaf on the ground.

"Yes, and I used to ask him just as I did you if he was glad he was a minister."

The man under the tree smiled a little sadly.

"Well — what did he say?"

"Oh, he always said he was, of course, but 'most always he said, too, that he wouldn't *stay* a minister a minute if 'twasn't for the rejoicing texts."

"The — *what?*" The Rev. Paul Ford's eyes left the leaf and gazed wonderingly into Pollyanna's merry little face.

"Well, that's what father used to call 'em," she laughed. "Of course the Bible didn't name 'em that. But it's all those that begin ' Be glad in the Lord,' or ' Rejoice greatly,' or ' Shout for joy,' and all that, you know — such a lot of 'em. Once, when father felt specially bad, he counted 'em. There were eight hundred of 'em."

"Eight hundred!"

"Yes — that told you to rejoice and be glad, you know; that's why father named 'em the ' rejoicing texts.' "

"Oh!" There was an odd look on the minister's face. His eyes had fallen to the words on the top paper in his hands — "But woe unto you, scribes and Pharisees, hypocrites!" "And so your father — liked those 'rejoicing texts,'" he murmured.

"Oh, yes," nodded Pollyanna, emphatically. "He said he felt better right away, that first day he thought to count 'em. He said if God took the trouble to tell us eight hundred times to be glad and rejoice, He must want us to do it — *some.* And father felt ashamed that he hadn't done it more. After that, they got to be such a comfort to him, you know, when things went wrong; when the Ladies' Aiders got to fight— I mean, when they *didn't agree* about something," corrected Pollyanna, hastily. "Why, it was those texts, too, father said, that made *him* think of the game — he began with *me* on the crutches — but he said 'twas the rejoicing texts that started him on it."

"And what game might that be?" asked the minister.

"About finding something in everything to be glad about, you know. As I said, he began with me on the crutches." And once more Pollyanna told her story — this time to a man who listened with tender eyes and understanding ears.

A little later Pollyanna and the minister descended the hill, hand in hand. Pollyanna's face

was radiant. Pollyanna loved to talk, and she had
been talking now for some time: there seemed to
be so many, many things about the game, her father,
and the old home life that the minister wanted to
know.

At the foot of the hill their ways parted, and
Pollyanna down one road, and the minister down
another, walked on alone.

In the Rev. Paul Ford's study that evening the
minister sat thinking. Near him on the desk lay
a few loose sheets of paper — his sermon notes.
Under the suspended pencil in his fingers lay other
sheets of paper, blank — his sermon to be. But the
minister was not thinking either of what he had
written, or of what he intended to write. In his
imagination he was far away in a little Western
town with a missionary minister who was poor,
sick, worried, and almost alone in the world — but
who was poring over the Bible to find how many
times his Lord and Master had told him to " rejoice and be glad."

After a time, with a long sigh, the Rev. Paul
Ford roused himself, came back from the far Western town, and adjusted the sheets of paper under
his hand.

" Matthew twenty-third; 13 — 14 and 23," he

wrote; then, with a gesture of impatience, he dropped his pencil and pulled toward him a magazine left on the desk by his wife a few minutes before. Listlessly his tired eyes turned from paragraph to paragraph until these words arrested them:

" A father one day said to his son, Tom, who, he knew, had refused to fill his mother's woodbox that morning: ' Tom, I'm sure you'll be glad to go and bring in some wood for your mother.' And without a word Tom went. Why? Just because his father showed so plainly that he expected him to do the right thing. Suppose he had said: ' Tom, I overheard what you said to your mother this morning, and I'm ashamed of you. Go at once and fill that woodbox!' I'll warrant that woodbox would be empty yet, so far as Tom was concerned!"

On and on read the minister — a word here, a line there, a paragraph somewhere else:

" What men and women need is encouragement. Their natural resisting powers should be strengthened, not weakened. . . . Instead of always harping on a man's faults, tell him of his virtues. Try to pull him out of his rut of bad habits. Hold up to him his better self, his *real* self that can dare and do and win out! . . . The influence of a beautiful, helpful, hopeful character is contagious, and may revolutionize a whole town. . . . People radiate what is in their minds and in their hearts. If a man feels kindly and obliging, his neighbors will feel that way, too, before long. But if he scolds and scowls and criticizes — his neighbors will return scowl for scowl, and add interest! . . . When you look for the bad, expecting it, you will get it. When you *know* you will find the good — you will get that. . . . Tell your son Tom you *know* he'll be glad to fill that woodbox — then watch him start, alert and interested!"

The minister dropped the paper and lifted his chin. In a moment he was on his feet, tramping the narrow room back and forth, back and forth. Later, some time later, he drew a long breath, and dropped himself in the chair at his desk.

"God helping me, I'll do it!" he cried softly. "I'll tell all my Toms I *know* they'll be glad to fill that woodbox! I'll give them work to do, and I'll make them so full of the very joy of doing it that they won't have *time* to look at their neighbors' woodboxes!" And he picked up his sermon notes, tore straight through the sheets, and cast them from him, so that on one side of his chair lay "But woe unto you," and on the other, "scribes and Pharisees, hypocrites!" while across the smooth white paper before him his pencil fairly flew — after first drawing one black line through " Matthew twenty-third; 13 — 14 and 23."

Thus it happened that the Rev. Paul Ford's sermon the next Sunday was a veritable bugle-call to the best that was in every man and woman and child that heard it; and its text was one of Pollyanna's shining eight hundred:

" Be glad in the Lord and rejoice, ye righteous, and shout for joy all ye that are upright in heart."

CHAPTER XXIII

AN ACCIDENT

AT Mrs. Snow's request, Pollyanna went one day to Dr. Chilton's office to get the name of a medicine which Mrs. Snow had forgotten. As it chanced, Pollyanna had never before seen the inside of Dr. Chilton's office.

"I've never been to your home before! This *is* your home, isn't it?" she said, looking interestedly about her.

The doctor smiled a little sadly.

"Yes — such as 'tis," he answered, as he wrote something on the pad of paper in his hand; "but it's a pretty poor apology for a home, Pollyanna. They're just rooms, that's all — not a home."

Pollyanna nodded her head wisely. Her eyes glowed with sympathetic understanding.

"I know. It takes a woman's hand and heart, or a child's presence to make a home," she said.

"Eh?" The doctor wheeled about abruptly.

"Mr. Pendleton told me," nodded Pollyanna,

229

again; "about the woman's hand and heart, or the child's presence, you know. Why don't you get a woman's hand and heart, Dr. Chilton? Or maybe you'd take Jimmy Bean — if Mr. Pendleton doesn't want him."

Dr. Chilton laughed a little constrainedly.

"So Mr. Pendleton says it takes a woman's hand and heart to make a home, does he?" he asked evasively.

"Yes. He says his is just a house, too. Why don't you, Dr. Chilton?"

"Why don't I — what?" The doctor had turned back to his desk.

"Get a woman's hand and heart. Oh — and I forgot." Pollyanna's face showed suddenly a painful color. "I suppose I ought to tell you. It wasn't Aunt Polly that Mr. Pendleton loved long ago; and so we — we aren't going there to live. You see, I told you it was — but I made a mistake. I hope *you* didn't tell any one," she finished anxiously.

"No — I didn't tell any one, Pollyanna," replied the doctor, a little queerly.

"Oh, that's all right, then," sighed Pollyanna in relief. "You see you're the only one I told, and I thought Mr. Pendleton looked sort of funny when I said I'd told *you*."

"Did he?" The doctor's lips twitched.

"Yes. And of course he wouldn't want many people to know it — when 'twasn't true. But why don't you get a woman's hand and heart, Dr. Chilton?"

There was a moment's silence; then very gravely the doctor said:

"They're not always to be had — for the asking, little girl."

Pollyanna frowned thoughtfully.

"But I should think *you* could get 'em," she argued. The flattering emphasis was unmistakable.

"Thank you," laughed the doctor, with uplifted eyebrows. Then, gravely again: "I'm afraid some of your older sisters would not be quite so — confident. At least, they — they haven't shown themselves to be so — obliging," he observed.

Pollyanna frowned again. Then her eyes widened in surprise.

"Why, Dr. Chilton, you don't mean — you didn't try to get somebody's hand and heart once, like Mr. Pendleton, and — and couldn't, did you?"

The doctor got to his feet a little abruptly.

"There, there, Pollyanna, never mind about that now. Don't let other people's troubles worry your little head. Suppose you run back now to Mrs.

Snow. I've written down the name of the medicine, and the directions how she is to take it. Was there anything else?"

Pollyanna shook her head.

"No, sir; thank you, sir," she murmured soberly, as she turned toward the door. From the little hallway she called back, her face suddenly alight: "Anyhow, I'm glad 'twasn't my mother's hand and heart that you wanted and couldn't get, Dr. Chilton. Good-by!"

It was on the last day of October that the accident occurred. Pollyanna, hurrying home from school, crossed the road at an apparently safe distance in front of a swiftly approaching motor car.

Just what happened, no one could seem to tell afterward. Neither was there any one found who could tell why it happened or who was to blame that it did happen. Pollyanna, however, at five o'clock, was borne, limp and unconscious, into the little room that was so dear to her. There, by a white-faced Aunt Polly and a weeping Nancy she was undressed tenderly and put to bed, while from the village, hastily summoned by telephone, Dr. Warren was hurrying as fast as another motor car could bring him.

"And ye didn't need ter more'n look at her aunt's face," Nancy was sobbing to Old Tom in the garden, after the doctor had arrived and was closeted in the hushed room; "ye didn't need ter more'n look at her aunt's face ter see that 'twa'n't no duty that was eatin' her. Yer hands don't shake, and yer eyes don't look as if ye was tryin' ter hold back the Angel o' Death himself, when you're jest doin' yer *duty*, Mr. Tom — they don't, they don't!"

"Is she hurt — bad?" The old man's voice shook.

"There ain't no tellin'," sobbed Nancy. "She lay back that white an' still she might easy be dead; but Miss Polly said she wa'n't dead — an' Miss Polly had oughter know, if any one would — she kept up such a listenin' an' a feelin' for her heartbeats an' her breath!"

"Couldn't ye tell anythin' what it done to her? — that — that —" Old Tom's face worked convulsively.

Nancy's lips relaxed a little.

"I wish ye *would* call it somethin', Mr. Tom — an' somethin' good an' strong, too. Drat it! Ter think of its runnin' down our little girl! I always hated the evil-smellin' things, anyhow — I did, I did!"

" But where is she hurt? "

" I don't know, I don't know," moaned Nancy. " There's a little cut on her blessed head, but 'tain't bad — that ain't — Miss Polly says. She says she's afraid it's infernally she's hurt."

A faint flicker came into Old Tom's eyes.

" I guess you mean in*ter*nally, Nancy," he said dryly. " She's hurt infernally, all right — plague take that autymobile! — but I don't guess Miss Polly'd be usin' that word, all the same."

" Eh? Well, I don't know, I don't know," moaned Nancy, with a shake of her head as she turned away. " Seems as if I jest couldn't stand it till that doctor gits out o' there. I wish I had a washin' ter do — the biggest washin' I ever see, I do, I do!" she wailed, wringing her hands helplessly.

Even after the doctor was gone, however, there seemed to be little that Nancy could tell Mr. Tom. There appeared to be no bones broken, and the cut was of slight consequence; but the doctor had looked very grave, had shaken his head slowly, and had said that time alone could tell. After he had gone, Miss Polly had shown a face even whiter and more drawn looking than before. The patient had not fully recovered consciousness, but at present she seemed to be resting as comfortably as could be expected. A trained nurse had been sent for, and would come that night. That was all. And Nancy turned sobbingly, and went back to her kitchen.

It was sometime during the next forenoon that Pollyanna opened conscious eyes and realized where she was.

"Why, Aunt Polly, what's the matter? Isn't it daytime? Why don't I get up?" she cried. "Why, Aunt Polly, I can't get up," she moaned, falling back on the pillow, after an ineffectual attempt to lift herself.

"No, dear, I wouldn't try — just yet," soothed her aunt quickly, but very quietly.

"But what is the matter? Why can't I get up?"

Miss Polly's eyes asked an agonized question of the white-capped young woman standing in the window, out of the range of Pollyanna's eyes.

The young woman nodded.

"Tell her," the lips said.

Miss Polly cleared her throat, and tried to swallow the lump that would scarcely let her speak.

"You were hurt, dear, by the automobile last night. But never mind that now. Auntie wants you to rest and go to sleep again."

"Hurt? Oh, yes; I — I ran." Pollyanna's eyes

were dazed. She lifted her hand to her forehead.
" Why, it's — done up, and it — hurts ! "

" Yes, dear; but never mind. Just — just rest."

" But, Aunt Polly, I feel so funny, and so bad !
My legs feel so — so queer — only they don't *feel*
— at all ! "

With an imploring look into the nurse's face,
Miss Polly struggled to her feet, and turned away.
The nurse came forward quickly.

" Suppose you let me talk to you now," she began cheerily. " I'm sure I think it's high time we
were getting acquainted, and I'm going to introduce
myself. I am Miss Hunt, and I've come to help
your aunt take care of you. And the very first thing
I'm going to do is to ask you to swallow these little
white pills for me."

Pollyanna's eyes grew a bit wild.

" But I don't want to be taken care of — that is,
not for long ! I want to get up. You know I go to
school. Can't I go to school to-morrow ? "

From the window where Aunt Polly stood now
there came a half-stifled cry.

" To-morrow ? " smiled the nurse, brightly.
" Well, I may not let you out quite so soon as that,
Miss Pollyanna. But just swallow these little pills
for me, please, and we'll see what *they'll* do."

"All right," agreed Pollyanna, somewhat doubtfully; "but I *must* go to school day after to-morrow — there are examinations then, you know."

She spoke again, a minute later. She spoke of school, and of the automobile, and of how her head ached; but very soon her voice trailed into silence under the blessed influence of the little white pills she had swallowed.

CHAPTER XXIV

JOHN PENDLETON

POLLYANNA did not go to school "to-morrow," nor the "day after to-morrow." Pollyanna, however, did not realize this, except momentarily when a brief period of full consciousness sent insistent questions to her lips. Pollyanna did not realize anything, in fact, very clearly until a week had passed; then the fever subsided, the pain lessened somewhat, and her mind awoke to full consciousness. She had then to be told all over again what had occurred.

"And so it's hurt that I am, and not sick," she sighed at last. "Well, I'm glad of that."

"G-glad, Pollyanna?" asked her aunt, who was sitting by the bed.

"Yes. I'd so much rather have broken legs like Mr. Pendleton's than life-long-invalids like Mrs. Snow, you know. Broken legs get well, and life-long-invalids don't."

Miss Polly — who had said nothing whatever about broken legs — got suddenly to her feet and walked to the little dressing table across the room. She was picking up one object after another now, and putting each down, in an aimless fashion quite unlike her usual decisiveness. Her face was not aimless-looking at all, however; it was white and drawn.

On the bed Pollyanna lay blinking at the dancing band of colors on the ceiling, which came from one of the prisms in the window.

"I'm glad it isn't smallpox that ails me, too," she murmured contentedly. "That would be worse than freckles. And I'm glad 'tisn't whooping cough — I've had that, and it's horrid — and I'm glad 'tisn't appendicitis nor measles, 'cause they're catching — measles are, I mean — and they wouldn't let you stay here."

"You seem to — to be glad for a good many things, my dear," faltered Aunt Polly, putting her hand to her throat as if her collar bound.

Pollyanna laughed softly.

"I am. I've been thinking of 'em — lots of 'em — all the time I've been looking up at that rainbow. I love rainbows. I'm so glad Mr. Pendleton gave me those prisms! I'm glad of some things I haven't said yet. I don't know but I'm 'most glad l was hurt."

" Pollyanna! "

Pollyanna laughed softly again. She turned luminous eyes on her aunt. " Well, you see, since I have been hurt, you've called me ' dear ' lots of times — and you didn't before. I love to be called ' dear ' — by folks that belong to you, I mean. Some of the Ladies' Aiders did call me that; and of course that was pretty nice, but not so nice as if they had belonged to me, like you do. Oh, Aunt Polly, I'm so glad you belong to me! "

Aunt Polly did not answer. Her hand was at her throat again. Her eyes were full of tears. She had turned away and was hurrying from the room through the door by which the nurse had just entered.

It was that afternoon that Nancy ran out to Old Tom, who was cleaning harnesses in the barn. Her eyes were wild.

" Mr. Tom, Mr. Tom, guess what's happened," sne panted. " You couldn't guess in a thousand years — you couldn't, you couldn't! "

" Then I cal'late I won't try," retorted the man, grimly, " specially as I hain't got more'n *ten* ter live, anyhow, probably. You'd better tell me first off, Nancy."

" Well, listen, then. Who do you s'pose is in the parlor now with the mistress? Who, I say? "

Old Tom shook his head.

" There's no tellin'," he declared.

" Yes, there is. I'm tellin'. It's — John Pendleton ! "

" Sho, now! You're jokin', girl."

" Not much I am — an' me a-lettin' him in myself — crutches an' all! An' the team he come in a-waitin' this minute at the door for him, jest as if he wa'n't the cranky old crosspatch he is, what never talks ter no one! Jest think, Mr. Tom — *him* a-callin' on *her!* "

" Well, why not? " demanded the old man, a little aggressively.

Nancy gave him a scornful glance.

" As if you didn't know better'n me! " she derided.

" Eh? "

" Oh, you needn't be so innercent," she retorted with mock indignation; " — you what led me wild-goose chasin' in the first place! "

" What do ye mean? "

Nancy glanced through the open barn door

toward the house, and came a step nearer to the old man.

"Listen! 'Twas you that was tellin' me Miss Polly had a lover in the first place, wa'n't it? Well, one day I thinks I finds two and two, and I puts 'em tergether an' makes four. But it turns out ter be five — an' no four at all, at all!"

With a gesture of indifference Old Tom turned and fell to work.

"If you're goin' ter talk ter me, you've got ter talk plain horse sense," he declared testily. "I never was no hand for figgers."

Nancy laughed.

"Well, it's this," she explained. "I heard some-thin' that made me think him an' Miss Polly was lovers."

"*Mr. Pendleton!*" Old Tom straightened up.

"Yes. Oh, I know now; he wasn't. It was that blessed child's mother he was in love with, and that's why he wanted — but never mind that part," she added hastily, remembering just in time her prom-ise to Pollyanna not to tell that Mr. Pendleton had wished her to come and live with him. "Well, I've been askin' folks about him some, since, and I've found out that him an' Miss Polly hain't been friends for years, an' that she's been hatin' him

like pizen owin' ter the silly gossip that coupled
their names tergether when she was eighteen or
twenty."

" Yes, I remember," nodded Old Tom. " It was
three or four years after Miss Jennie give him the
mitten and went off with the other chap. Miss
Polly knew about it, of course, and was sorry for
him. So she tried ter be nice to him. Maybe she
overdid it a little — she hated that minister chap
so who had took off her sister. At any rate, somebody begun ter make trouble. They said she was
runnin' after him."

" Runnin' after any man — her! " interjected
Nancy.

" I know it; but they did," declared Old Tom,
" and of course no gal of any spunk'll stand that.
Then about that time come her own lover an' the
trouble with *him*. After that she shut up like an
oyster an' wouldn't have nothin' ter do with nobody
fur a spell. Her heart jest seemed to turn bitter at
the core."

" Yes, I know. I've heard about that now," rejoined Nancy; " an' that's why you could 'a'
knocked me down with a feather when I see *him*
at the door — him, what she hain't spoke to for
years! But I let him in an' went an' told her."

"What did she say?" Old Tom held his breath suspended.

"Nothin' — at first. She was so still I thought she hadn't heard; and I was jest goin' ter say it over when she speaks up quiet like: 'Tell Mr. Pendleton I will be down at once.' An' I come an' told him. Then I come out here an' told you," finished Nancy, casting another backward glance toward the house.

"Humph!" grunted Old Tom; and fell to work again.

In the ceremonious "parlor" of the Harrington homestead, Mr. John Pendleton did not have to wait long before a swift step warned him of Miss Polly's coming. As he attempted to rise, she made a gesture of remonstrance. She did not offer her hand, however, and her face was coldly reserved.

"I called to ask for — Pollyanna," he began at once, a little brusquely.

"Thank you. She is about the same," said Miss Polly.

"And that is — won't you tell me *how* she is?" His voice was not quite steady this time.

A quick spasm of pain crossed the woman's face.

"I can't, I wish I could!"

"You mean — you don't know?"

"Yes."

"But — the doctor?"

"Dr. Warren himself seems — at sea. He is in correspondence now with a New York specialist. They have arranged for a consultation — at once."

"But — but what *were* her injuries that you do know?"

"A slight cut on the head, one or two bruises, and — and an injury to the spine which has seemed to cause — paralysis from the hips down."

A low cry came from the man. There was a brief silence; then, huskily, he asked:

"And Pollyanna — how does she — take it?"

"She doesn't understand — at all — how things really are. And I *can't* tell her."

"But she must know — something!"

Miss Polly lifted her hand to the collar at her throat in the gesture that had become so common to her of late.

"Oh, yes. She knows she can't — move; but she thinks her legs are — broken. She says she's glad it's broken legs like yours rather than 'life-long-invalids' like Mrs. Snow's; because broken legs get well and the other — doesn't. She talks like that all the time, until it — it seems as if I should — die!"

Through the blur of tears in his own eyes, the man saw the drawn face opposite, twisted with emotion. Involuntarily his thoughts went back to what Pollyanna had said when he had made his final plea for her presence: " Oh, I couldn't leave Aunt Polly — now!"

It was this thought that made him ask very gently, as soon as he could control his voice:

" I wonder if you know, Miss Harrington, how hard I tried to get Pollyanna to come and live with me."

" With *you!* — Pollyanna!"

The man winced a little at the tone of her voice; but his own voice was still impersonally cool when he spoke again.

" Yes. I wanted to adopt her — legally, you understand; making her my heir, of course."

The woman in the opposite chair relaxed a little. It came to her, suddenly, what a brilliant future it would have meant for Pollyanna — this adoption; and she wondered if Pollyanna were old enough — and mercenary enough — to be tempted by this man's money and position.

" I am very fond of Pollyanna," the man was

continuing. "I am fond of her both for her own sake, and for — her mother's. I stood ready to give Pollyanna the love that had been twenty-five years in storage."

"*Love.*" Miss Polly remembered suddenly why *she* had taken this child in the first place — and with the recollection came the remembrance of Pollyanna's own words uttered that very morning: "I love to be called 'dear' by folks that belong to you!" And it was this love-hungry little girl that had been offered the stored-up affection of twenty-five years: — and she *was* old enough to be tempted by love! With a sinking heart Miss Polly realized that. With a sinking heart, too, she realized something else: the dreariness of her own future now — without Pollyanna.

"Well?" she said. And the man, recognizing the self-control that vibrated through the harshness of the tone, smiled sadly.

"She would not come," he answered.

"Why?"

"She would not leave you. She said you had been so good to her. She wanted to stay with you — and she said she *thought* you wanted her to stay," he finished, as he pulled himself to his feet.

He did not look toward Miss Polly. He turned

his face resolutely toward the door. But instantly he heard a swift step at his side, and found a shaking hand thrust toward him.

"When the specialist comes, and I know any-thing — definite about Pollyanna, I will let you hear from me," said a trembling voice. "Good-by — and thank you for coming. Pollyanna will be — pleased."

CHAPTER XXV

A WAITING GAME

On the day after John Pendleton's call at the Harrington homestead, Miss Polly set herself to the task of preparing Pollyanna for the visit of the specialist.

"Pollyanna, my dear," she began gently, "we have decided that we want another doctor besides Dr. Warren to see you. Another one might tell us something new to do — to help you get well faster, you know."

A joyous light came to Pollyanna's face.

"Dr. Chilton! Oh, Aunt Polly, I'd so love to have Dr. Chilton! I've wanted him all the time, but I was afraid you didn't, on account of his seeing you in the sun parlor that day, you know; so I didn't like to say anything. But I'm so glad you do want him!"

Aunt Polly's face had turned white, then red, then back to white again. But when she answered, she showed very plainly that she was trying to speak lightly and cheerfully.

" Oh, no, dear! It wasn't Dr. Chilton at all that I meant. It is a new doctor — a very famous doctor from New York, who — who knows a great deal about — about hurts like yours."

Pollyanna's face fell.

" I don't believe he knows half so much as Dr. Chilton."

" Oh, yes, he does, I'm sure, dear."

" But it was Dr. Chilton who doctored Mr. Pendleton's broken leg, Aunt Polly. If — if you don't mind *very* much, I *would like* to have Dr. Chilton — truly I would! "

A distressed color suffused Miss Polly's face. For a moment she did not speak at all; then she said gently — though yet with a touch of her old stern decisiveness:

" But I do mind, Pollyanna. I mind very much. I would do anything — almost anything for you, my dear; but I — for reasons which I do not care to speak of now, I don't wish Dr. Chilton called in on — on this case. And believe me, he can *not* know so much about — about your trouble, as this great doctor does, who will come from New York to-morrow."

Pollyanna still looked unconvinced.

"But, Aunt Polly, if you *loved* Dr. Chilton — "

"*What*, Pollyanna?" Aunt Polly's voice was very sharp now. Her cheeks were very red, too.

"I say, if you loved Dr. Chilton, and didn't love the other one," sighed Pollyanna, "seems to me that would make some difference in the good he would do; and I love Dr. Chilton."

The nurse entered the room at that moment, and Aunt Polly rose to her feet abruptly, a look of relief on her face.

"I am very sorry, Pollyanna," she said, a little stiffly; "but I'm afraid you'll have to let me be the judge, this time. Besides, it's already arranged. The New York doctor is coming to-morrow."

As it happened, however, the New York doctor did not come "to-morrow." At the last moment a telegram told of an unavoidable delay owing to the sudden illness of the specialist himself. This led Pollyanna into a renewed pleading for the substitution of Dr. Chilton — "which would be so easy now, you know."

But as before, Aunt Polly shook her head and said "no, dear," very decisively, yet with a still more anxious assurance that she would do anything

— anything but that — to please her dear Pollyanna.

As the days of waiting passed, one by one, it did
indeed, seem that Aunt Polly was doing everything
(but that) that she could do to please her niece.

"I wouldn't 'a' believed it — you couldn't 'a'
made me believe it," Nancy said to Old Tom one
morning. "There don't seem ter be a minute in
the day that Miss Polly ain't jest hangin' 'round
waitin' ter do somethin' for that blessed lamb, if
'tain't more than ter let in the cat — an' her what
wouldn't let Fluff nor Buff up-stairs for love nor
money a week ago; an' now she lets 'em tumble
all over the bed jest 'cause it pleases Miss Pollyanna!

"An' when she ain't doin' nothin' else, she's
movin' them little glass danglers 'round ter diff'-
rent winders in the room so the sun'll make the
'rainbows dance,' as that blessed child calls it.
She's sent Timothy down ter Cobb's greenhouse
three times for fresh flowers — an' that besides all
the posies fetched in ter her, too. An' the other
day, if I didn't find her sittin' 'fore the bed with
the nurse actually doin' her hair, an' Miss Pollyanna lookin' on an' bossin' from the bed, her eyes
all shinin' an' happy. An' I declare ter goodness, if

Miss Polly hain't wore her hair like that every day now — jest ter please that blessed child!"

Old Tom chuckled.

"Well, it strikes me Miss Polly herself ain't lookin' none the worse — for wearin' them 'ere curls 'round her forehead," he observed dryly.

"'Course she ain't," retorted Nancy, indignantly. "She looks like *folks,* now. She's actually almost — "

"Keerful, now, Nancy!" interrupted the old man, with a slow grin. "You know what you said when I told ye she was handsome once."

Nancy shrugged her shoulders.

"Oh, she ain't handsome, of course; but I will own up she don't look like the same woman, what with the ribbons an' lace jiggers Miss Pollyanna makes her wear 'round her neck."

"I told ye so," nodded the man. "I told ye she wa'n't — old."

Nancy laughed.

"Well, I'll own up she *hain't* got quite so good an imitation of it — as she did have, 'fore Miss Pollyanna come. Say, Mr. Tom, who *was* her lover? I hain't found that out, yet; I hain't, I hain't!"

"Hain't ye?" asked the old man, with an odd

look on his face. "Well, I guess ye won't then —
from me."

"Oh, Mr. Tom, come on, now," wheedled the
girl. "Ye see, there ain't many folks here that I
can ask."

"Maybe not. But there's one, anyhow, that
ain't answerin'," grinned Old Tom. Then, abruptly, the light died from his eyes. "How is she,
ter-day — the little gal?"

Nancy shook her head. Her face, too, had so-
bered.

"Just the same, Mr. Tom. There ain't no special
diff'rence, as I can see — or anybody, I guess. She
jest lays there an' sleeps an' talks some, an' tries
ter smile an' be 'glad' 'cause the sun sets or the
moon rises, or some other such thing, till it's enough
ter make yer heart break with achin'."

"I know; it's the 'game' — bless her sweet
heart!" nodded Old Tom, blinking a little.

"She told *you*, then, too, about that 'ere —
game?"

"Oh, yes. She told me long ago." The old man
hesitated, then went on, his lips twitching a little.
"I was growlin' one day 'cause I was so bent up
and crooked; an' what do ye s'pose the little thing
said?"

"I couldn't guess. I wouldn't think she could find *anythin'* about *that* ter be glad about!"

"She did. She said I could be glad, anyhow, that I didn't have ter *stoop so far ter do my weedin'* — 'cause I was already bent part way over."

Nancy gave a wistful laugh.

"Well, I ain't surprised, after all. You might know she'd find somethin'. We've been playin' it — that game — since almost the first, 'cause there wa'n't no one else she could play it with — though she did speak of — her aunt."

"*Miss Polly!*"

Nancy chuckled.

"I guess you hain't got such an awful diff'rent opinion o' the mistress than I have," she bridled.

Old Tom stiffened.

"I was only thinkin' 'twould be — some of a surprise - to her," he explained with dignity.

"Well, yes, I guess 'twould be — *then*," retorted Nancy. "I ain't sayin' what 'twould be *now*. I'd believe anythin' o' the mistress now — even that she'd take ter playin' it herself!"

"But hain't the little gal told her — ever? She's told ev'ry one else, I guess. I'm hearin' of it ev'rywhere, now, since she was hurted," said Tom.

"Well, she didn't tell Miss Polly," rejoined

Nancy. " Miss Pollyanna told me long ago that she couldn't tell her, 'cause her aunt didn't like ter have her talk about her father; an' 'twas her father's game, an' she'd have ter talk about him if she did tell it. So she never told her."

" Oh, I see, I see." The old man nodded his head slowly. " They was always bitter against the minister chap — all of 'em, 'cause he took Miss Jennie away from 'em. An' Miss Polly — young as she was — couldn't never forgive him; she was that fond of Miss Jennie — in them days. I see, I see. 'Twas a bad mess," he sighed, as he turned away.

" Yes, 'twas — all 'round, all 'round," sighed Nancy in her turn, as she went back to her kitchen.

For no one were those days of waiting easy. The nurse tried to look cheerful, but her eyes were troubled. The doctor was openly nervous and impatient. Miss Polly said little; but even the softening waves of hair about her face, and the becoming laces at her throat, could not hide the fact that she was growing thin and pale. As to Pollyanna — Pollyanna petted the dog, smoothed the cat's sleek head, admired the flowers and ate the fruits and jellies that were sent in to her; and returned innumerable cheery answers to the many messages of love and inquiry that were brought to her bedside. But she, too, grew pale and thin; and the nervous activity of the poor little hands and arms only emphasized the pitiful motionlessness of the once active little feet and legs now lying so woefully quiet under the blankets.

As to the game — Pollyanna told Nancy these days how glad she was going to be when she could go to school again, go to see Mrs. Snow, go to call on Mr. Pendleton, and go to ride with Dr. Chilton; nor did she seem to realize that all this " gladness " was in the future, not the present. Nancy, however, did realize it — and cry about it, when she was alone.

CHAPTER XXVI

A DOOR AJAR

Just a week from the time Dr. Mead, the specialist, was first expected, he came. He was a tall,
broad-shouldered man with kind gray eyes, and a
cheerful smile. Pollyanna liked him at once, and
told him so.

"You look quite a lot like *my* doctor, you see,"
she added engagingly.

"*Your* doctor?" Dr. Mead glanced in evident
surprise at Dr. Warren, talking with the nurse a
few feet away. Dr. Warren was a small, brown-
eyed man with a pointed brown beard.

"Oh, *that* isn't my doctor," smiled Pollyanna,
divining his thought. "Dr. Warren is Aunt Polly's
doctor. My doctor is Dr. Chilton."

"Oh-h!" said Dr. Mead, a little oddly, his eyes
resting on Miss Polly, who, with a vivid blush, had
turned hastily away.

"Yes." Pollyanna hesitated, then continued
with her usual truthfulness. "You see, *I* wanted
Dr. Chilton all the time, but Aunt Polly wanted

you. She said you knew more than Dr. Chilton, anyway about — about broken legs like mine. And of course if you do, I can be glad for that. Do you?"

A swift something crossed the doctor's face that Pollyanna could not quite translate.

"Only time can tell that, little girl," he said gently; then he turned a grave face toward Dr. Warren, who had just come to the bedside.

Every one said afterward that it was the cat that did it. Certainly, if Fluffy had not poked an insistent paw and nose against Pollyanna's unlatched door, the door would not have swung noiselessly open on its hinges until it stood perhaps a foot ajar; and if the door had not been open, Pollyanna would not have heard her aunt's words.

In the hall the two doctors, the nurse, and Miss Polly stood talking. In Pollyanna's room Fluffy had just jumped to the bed with a little purring "meow" of joy when through the open door sounded clearly and sharply Aunt Polly's agonized exclamation.

"Not that! Doctor, not that! You don't mean — the child — will *never walk* again!"

It was all confusion then. First, from the bed-

room came Pollyanna's terrified " Aunt Polly —
Aunt Polly!" Then Miss Polly, seeing the open
door and realizing that her words had been heard,
gave a low little moan and — for the first time in
her life — fainted dead away.

The nurse, with a choking " She heard!" stumbled toward the open door. The two doctors stayed
with Miss Polly. Dr. Mead had to stay — he had
caught Miss Polly as she fell. Dr. Warren stood
by, helplessly. It was not until Pollyanna cried out
again sharply and the nurse closed the door, that
the two men, with a despairing glance into each
other's eyes, awoke to the immediate duty of bring-
ing the woman in Dr. Mead's arms back to unhappy
consciousness.

In Pollyanna's room, the nurse had found a purring gray cat on the bed vainly trying to attract the
attention of a white-faced, wild-eyed little girl.

" Miss Hunt, please, I want Aunt Polly. I want
her right away, quick, please!"

The nurse closed the door and came forward hurriedly. Her face was very pale.

" She — she can't come just this minute, dear.
She will — a little later. What is it? Can't I —
get it?"

Pollyanna shook her head.

" But I want to know what she said — just now. Did you hear her? I want Aunt Polly — she said something. I want her to tell me 'tisn't true — 'tisn't true ! "

The nurse tried to speak, but no words came. Something in her face sent an added terror to Pollyanna's eyes.

" Miss Hunt, you *did* hear her! It *is* true! Oh, it *isn't* true! You don't mean I can't ever — walk again? "

" There, there, dear — don't, don't! " choked the nurse. " Perhaps he didn't know. Perhaps he was mistaken. There's lots of things that could happen, you know."

" But Aunt Polly said he did know! She said he knew more than anybody else about — about broken legs like mine! "

" Yes, yes, I know, dear; but all doctors make mistakes sometimes. Just — just don't think any more about it now — please don't, dear."

Pollyanna flung out her arms wildly.

" But I can't help thinking about it," she sobbed. " It's all there is now to think about. Why, Miss Hunt, how am I going to school, or to see Mr. Pendleton, or Mrs. Snow, or — or anybody? " She caught her breath and sobbed wildly for a moment. Suddenly she stopped and looked up, a new terror in her eyes. "Why, Miss Hunt, if I can't walk, how am I ever going to be glad for — *anything?*"

Miss Hunt did not know "the game;" but she did know that her patient must be quieted, and that at once. In spite of her own perturbation and heartache, her hands had not been idle, and she stood now at the bedside with the quieting powder ready.

"There, there, dear, just take this," she soothed; "and by and by we'll be more rested, and we'll see what can be done then. Things aren't half as bad as they seem, dear, lots of times, you know."

Obediently Pollyanna took the medicine, and sipped the water from the glass in Miss Hunt's hand.

"I know; that sounds like things father used to say," faltered Pollyanna, blinking off the tears. "He said there was always something about everything that might be worse; but I reckon he'd never just heard he couldn't ever walk again. I don't see how there *can* be anything about that, that could be worse — do you?"

Miss Hunt did not reply. She could not trust herself to speak just then.

CHAPTER XXVII

TWO VISITS

IT was Nancy who was sent to tell Mr. John Pendleton of Dr. Mead's verdict. Miss Polly had remembered her promise to let him have direct information from the house. To go herself, or to write a letter, she felt to be almost equally out of the question. It occurred to her then to send Nancy.

There had been a time when Nancy would have rejoiced greatly at this extraordinary opportunity to see something of the House of Mystery and its master. But to-day her heart was too heavy to rejoice at anything. She scarcely even looked about her at all, indeed, during the few minutes she waited for Mr. John Pendleton to appear.

"I'm Nancy, sir," she said respectfully, in response to the surprised questioning of his eyes, when he came into the room. "Miss Harrington sent me to tell you about — Miss Pollyanna."

"Well?"

In spite of the curt terseness of the word, Nancy quite understood the anxiety that lay behind that short " well? "

" It ain't well, Mr. Pendleton," she choked.

" You don't mean — " He paused, and she bowed her head miserably.

" Yes, sir. He says — she can't walk again — never."

For a moment there was absolute silence in the room; then the man spoke, in a voice shaken with emotion.

" Poor — little — girl! Poor — little — girl! "

Nancy glanced at him, but dropped her eyes at once. She had not supposed that sour, cross, stern John Pendleton could look like that. In a moment he spoke again, still in the low, unsteady voice.

" It seems cruel — never to dance in the sunshine again! My little prism girl! "

There was another silence; then, abruptly, the man asked:

" She herself doesn't know yet — of course — does she? "

" But she does, sir." sobbed Nancy: " an' that's what makes it all the harder. She found out — drat that cat! I begs yer pardon," apologized the girl, hurriedly. " It's only that the cat pushed open the door an' Miss Pollyanna overheard 'em talkin'. She found out — that way."

" Poor — little — girl!" sighed the man again.

"Yes, sir. You'd say so, sir, if you could see her," choked Nancy. "I hain't seen her but twice since she knew about it, an' it done me up both times. Ye see it's all so fresh an' new to her, an' she keeps thinkin' all the time of new things she can't do — now. It worries her, too, 'cause she can't seem ter be glad — maybe you don't know about her game, though," broke off Nancy, apologetically.

"The 'glad game'?" asked the man. "Oh, yes; she told me of that."

"Oh, she did! Well, I guess she has told it generally ter most folks. But ye see, now she — she can't play it herself, an' it worries her. She says she can't think of a thing — not a thing about this not walkin' again, ter be glad about."

"Well, why should she?" retorted the man, almost savagely.

Nancy shifted her feet uneasily.

"That's the way I felt, too — till I happened ter think — it *would* be easier if she *could* find somethin', ye know. So I tried to — to remind her."

"To remind her! Of what?" John Pendleton's voice was still angrily impatient.

"Of — of how she told others ter play it — Mis' Snow, and the rest, ye know — and what she said for them ter do. But the poor little lamb just cries, an' says it don't seem the same, somehow. She says it's easy ter *tell* lifelong invalids how ter be glad, but 'tain't the same thing when you'.e the lifelong invalid yerself, an' have ter try ter do it. She says she's told herself over an' over again how glad she is that other folks ain't like her; but that all the time she's sayin' it, she ain't really *thinkin'* of anythin' only how she can't ever walk again."

Nancy paused, but the man did not speak. He sat with his hand over his eyes.

"Then I tried ter remind her how she used ter say the game was all the nicer ter play when — when it was hard," resumed Nancy, in a dull voice. "But she says that, too, is diff'rent — when it really *is* hard. An' I must be goin', now, sir," she broke off abruptly.

At the door she hesitated, turned, and asked timidly:

"I couldn't be tellin' Miss Pollyanna that — that you'd seen Jimmy Bean again, I s'pose, sir, could I?"

" I don't see how you could — as I haven't seen him," observed the man a little shortly. " Why?"

" Nothin', sir, only — well, ye see, that's one of the things that she was feelin' bad about, that she couldn't take him ter see you, now. She said she'd taken him once, but she didn't think he showed off very well that day, and that she was afraid you didn't think he would make a very nice child's presence, after all. Maybe you know what she means by that; but I didn't, sir."

" Yes, I know — what she means."

" All right, sir. It was only that she was wantin' ter take him again, she said, so's ter show ye he really was a lovely child's presence. And now she — can't! — drat that autymobile! I begs yer pardon, sir. Good-by!" And Nancy fled precipitately.

It did not take long for the entire town of Beldingsville to learn that the great New York doctor had said Pollyanna Whittier would never walk again; and certainly never before had the town been so stirred. Everybody knew by sight now the piquant little freckled face that had always a smile of greeting; and almost everybody knew of the " game " that Pollyanna was playing. To think that now never again would that smiling face be seen on their streets — never again would that cheery little voice proclaim the gladness of some everyday experience! It seemed unbelievable, impossible, cruel.

In kitchens and sitting rooms, and over back--yard fences women talked of it, and wept openly. On street corners and in store lounging-places the men talked, too, and wept — though not so openly. And neither the talking nor the weeping grew less when fast on the heels of the news itself, came Nancy's pitiful story that Pollyanna, face to face with what had come to her, was bemoaning most of all the fact that she could not play the game; that she could not now be glad over — anything.

It was then that the same thought must have, in some way, come to Pollyanna's friends. At all events, almost at once, the mistress of the Harrington homestead, greatly to her surprise, began to receive calls: calls from people she knew, and people she did not know; calls from men, women, and children — many of whom Miss Polly had not supposed that her niece knew at all.

Some came in and sat down for a stiff five or ten minutes. Some stood awkwardly on the porch steps, fumbling with hats or hand-bags, according to their sex. Some brought a book, a bunch of flowers, or a dainty to tempt the palate. Some cried frankly. Some turned their backs and blew their noses furiously. But all inquired very anxiously for the little injured girl; and all sent to her some message — and it was these messages which, after a time, stirred Miss Polly to action.

First came Mr. John Pendleton. He came without his crutches to-day.

" I don't need to tell you how shocked I am," he began almost harshly. " But can — nothing be done? "

Miss Polly gave a gesture of despair.

" Oh, we're ' doing,' of course, all the time. Dr. Mead prescribed certain treatments and medicines that might help, and Dr. Warren is carrying them out to the letter, of course. But — Dr. Mead held out almost no hope."

John Pendleton rose abruptly — though he had but just come. His face was white, and his mouth was set into stern lines. Miss Polly, looking at him, knew very well why he felt that he could not stay longer in her presence. At the door he turned.

" I have a message for Pollyanna," he said. " Will you tell her, please, that I have seen Jimmy Bean and—that he's going to be my boy hereafter.

Tell her I thought she would be — *glad* to know. I shall adopt him, probably."

For a brief moment Miss Polly lost her usual well-bred self-control.

" You will adopt Jimmy Bean!" she gasped.

The man lifted his chin a little.

" Yes. I think Pollyanna will understand. You will tell her I thought she would be — *glad?*"

" Why, of — of course," faltered Miss Polly.

" Thank you," bowed John Pendleton, as he turned to go.

In the middle of the floor Miss Polly stood, silent and amazed, still looking after the man who had just left her. Even yet she could scarcely believe what her ears had heard. John Pendleton *adopt* Jimmy Bean? John Pendleton, wealthy, independent, morose, reputed to be miserly and supremely selfish, to adopt a little boy — and such a little boy?

With a somewhat dazed face Miss Polly went up-stairs to Pollyanna's room.

" Pollyanna, I have a message for you from Mr. John Pendleton. He has just been here. He says to tell you he has taken Jimmy Bean for his little boy. He said he thought you'd be glad to know it."

Pollyanna's wistful little face flamed into sudden joy.

"Glad? *Glad?* Well, I reckon I am glad! Oh, Aunt Polly, I've so wanted to find a place for Jimmy — and that's such a lovely place! Besides, I'm so glad for Mr. Pendleton, too. You see, now he'll have the child's presence."

" The — what? "

Pollyanna colored painfully. She had forgotten that she had never told her aunt of Mr. Pendleton's desire to adopt her — and certainly she would not wish to tell her now that she had ever thought for a minute of leaving her — this dear Aunt Polly!

" The child's presence," stammered Pollyanna, hastily. "Mr. Pendleton told me once, you see, that only a woman's hand and heart or a child's presence could make a — a home. And now he's got it — the child's presence."

" Oh, I — see," said Miss Polly very gently; and she did see — more than Pollyanna realized. She saw something of the pressure that was probably brought to bear on Pollyanna herself at the time John Pendleton was asking *her* to be the " child's presence," which was to transform his great pile of gray stone into a home. " I see," she finished, her eyes stinging with sudden tears.

Pollyanna, fearful that her aunt might ask further embarrassing questions, hastened to lead the conversation away from the Pendleton house and its master.

"Dr. Chilton says so, too — that it takes a woman's hand and heart, or a child's presence, to make a home, you know," she remarked.

Miss Polly turned with a start.

"*Dr. Chilton!* How do you know — that?"

"He told me so. 'Twas when he said he lived in just rooms, you know — not a home."

Miss Polly did not answer. Her eyes were out the window.

"So I asked him why he didn't get 'em — a woman's hand and heart, and have a home."

"Pollyanna!" Miss Polly had turned sharply. Her cheeks showed a sudden color.

"Well, I did. He looked so — so sorrowful."

"What did he — say?" Miss Polly asked the question as if in spite of some force within her that was urging her not to ask it.

"He didn't say anything for a minute; then he said very low that you couldn't always get 'em for the asking."

There was a brief silence. Miss Polly's eyes had

turned again to the window. Her cheeks were still unnaturally pink.

Pollyanna sighed.

"He wants one, anyhow, I know, and I wish he could have one."

"Why, Pollyanna, *how* do you know?"

"Because, afterwards, on another day, he said something else. He said that low, too, but I heard him. He said that he'd give all the world if he did have one woman's hand and heart. Why, Aunt Polly, what's the matter?" Aunt Polly had risen hurriedly and gone to the window.

"Nothing, dear. I was changing the position of this prism," said Aunt Polly, whose whole face now was aflame.

CHAPTER XXVIII

THE GAME AND ITS PLAYERS

It was not long after John Pendleton's second visit that Milly Snow called one afternoon. Milly Snow had never before been to the Harrington homestead. She blushed and looked very embarrassed when Miss Polly entered the room.

"I — I came to inquire for the little girl," she stammered.

"You are very kind. She is about the same. How is your mother?" rejoined Miss Polly, wearily.

"That is what I came to tell you — that is, to ask you to tell Miss Pollyanna," hurried on the girl, breathlessly and incoherently. "We think it's — so awful — so perfectly awful that the little thing can't ever walk again; and after all she's done for us, too — for mother, you know, teaching her to play the game, and all that. And when we heard how now she couldn't play it herself — poor little dear! I'm sure I don't see how she *can*, either, in her condition! — but when we remembered all the things she'd said to us, we thought if she could only know what she *had* done for us, that it would *help,* you know, in her own case, about the game, because she could be glad — that is, a little glad — " Milly stopped helplessly, and seemed to be waiting for Miss Polly to speak.

Miss Polly had sat politely listening, but with a puzzled questioning in her eyes. Only about half of what had been said, had she understood. She was thinking now that she always had known that Milly Snow was " queer," but she had not supposed she was crazy. In no other way, however, could she account for this incoherent, illogical, unmeaning rush of words. When the pause came she filled it with a quiet:

" I don't think I quite understand, Milly. Just what is it that you want me to tell my niece? "

" Yes, that's it; I want you to tell her," answered the girl, feverishly. " Make her see what she's done for us. Of course she's *seen* some things, because she's been there, and she's known mother is different; but I want her to know *how* different she is — and me, too. I'm different. I've been trying to play it — the game — a little."

Miss Polly frowned. She would have asked what Milly meant by this " game," but there was no opportunity. Milly was rushing on again with nervous volubility.

"You know nothing was ever right before — for mother. She was always wanting 'em different. And, really, I don't know as one could blame her much — under the circumstances. But now she lets me keep the shades up, and she takes interest in things — how she looks, and her nightdress, and all that. And she's actually begun to knit little things — reins and baby blankets for fairs and hospitals. And she's so interested, and so *glad* to think she can do it! — and that was all Miss Polly- anna's doings, you know, 'cause she told mother she could be glad she'd got her hands and arms, anyway; and that made mother wonder right away why she didn't *do* something with her hands and arms. And so she began to do something — to knit, you know. And you can't think what a dif- ferent room it is now, what with the red and blue and yellow worsteds, and the prisms in the win- dow that *she* gave her — why, it actually makes you feel *better* just to go in there now; and before I used to dread it awfully, it was so dark and gloomy, and mother was so — so unhappy. you know.

"And so we want you to please tell Miss Pollyanna that we understand it's all because of her. And please say we're so glad we know her, that we thought, maybe if she knew it, it would make her a little glad that she knew us. And — and that's all," sighed Milly, rising hurriedly to her feet. "You'll tell her?"

"Why, of course," murmured Miss Polly, wondering just how much of this remarkable discourse she could remember to tell.

These visits of John Pendleton and Milly Snow were only the first of many; and always there were the messages — the messages which were in some ways so curious that they caused Miss Polly more and more to puzzle over them.

One day there was the little Widow Benton. Miss Polly knew her well, though they had never called upon each other. By reputation she knew her as the saddest little woman in town — one who was always in black. To-day, however, Mrs. Benton wore a knot of pale blue at the throat, though there were tears in her eyes. She spoke of her grief and horror at the accident; then she asked diffidently if she might see Pollyanna.

Miss Polly shook her head.

"I am sorry, but she sees no one yet. A little later — perhaps."

Mrs. Benton wiped her eyes, rose, and turned to go. But after she had almost reached the hall door she came back hurriedly.

"Miss Harrington, perhaps you'd give her — a message," she stammered.

"Certainly, Mrs. Benton; I shall be very glad to."

Still the little woman hesitated; then she spoke.

"Will you tell her, please, that — that I've put on *this*," she said, just touching the blue bow at her throat. Then, at Miss Polly's ill-concealed look of surprise, she added: "The little girl has been trying for so long to make me wear — some color, that I thought she'd be — glad to know I'd begun. She said that Freddy would be so glad to see it, if I would. You know Freddy's *all* I have now. The others have all — " Mrs. Benton shook her head and turned away. "If you'll just tell Polly-anna — *she'll* understand." And the door closed after her.

A little later, that same day, there was the other widow — at least, she wore widow's garments. Miss Polly did not know her at all. She wondered vaguely how Pollyanna could have known her. The lady gave her name as "Mrs. Tarbell."

"I'm a stranger to you, of course," she began

at once. "But I'm not a stranger to your little niece, Pollyanna. I've been at the hotel all summer, and every day I've had to take long walks for my health. It was on these walks that I've met your niece — she's such a dear little girl! I wish I could make you understand what she's been to me. I was very sad when I came up here; and her bright face and cheery ways reminded me of — my own little girl that I lost years ago. I was so shocked to hear of the accident; and then when I learned that the poor child would never walk again, and that she was so unhappy because she couldn't be glad any longer — the dear child! — I just had to come to you."

"You are very kind," murmured Miss Polly.

"But it is you who are to be kind," demurred the other. "I — I want you to give her a message from me. Will you?"

"Certainly."

"Will you just tell her, then, that Mrs. Tarbell is glad now. Yes, I know it sounds odd, and you don't understand. But — if you'll pardon me I'd rather not explain." Sad lines came to the lady's mouth, and the smile left her eyes. "Your niece will know just what I mean; and I felt that I must tell — her. Thank you; and pardon me, please, for any seeming rudeness in my call," she begged, as she took her leave.

Thoroughly mystified now, Miss Polly hurried up-stairs to Pollyanna's room.

" Pollyanna, do you know a Mrs. Tarbell? "

" Oh, yes. I love Mrs. Tarbell. She's sick, and awfully sad; and she's at the hotel, and takes long walks. We go together. I mean — we used to." Pollyanna's voice broke, and two big tears rolled down her cheeks.

Miss Polly cleared her throat hurriedly.

" Well, she's just been here, dear. She left a message for you — but she wouldn't tell me what it meant. She said to tell you that Mrs. Tarbell is glad now."

Pollyanna clapped her hands softly.

" Did she say that — really? Oh, I'm so glad! "

" But, Pollyanna, what did she mean? "

" Why, it's the game, and — " Pollyanna stopped short, her fingers to her lips.

" What game? "

" N-nothing much, Aunt Polly; that is — I can't tell it unless I tell other things that — that I'm not to speak of."

It was on Miss Polly's tongue to question her niece further; but the obvious distress on the little girl's face stayed the words before they were uttered.

Not long after Mrs. Tarbell's visit, the climax came. It came in the shape of a call from a certain young woman with unnaturally pink cheeks and abnormally yellow hair; a young woman who wore high heels and cheap jewelry; a young woman whom Miss Polly knew very well by reputation — but whom she was angrily amazed to meet beneath the roof of the Harrington homestead.

Miss Polly did not offer her hand. She drew back, indeed, as she entered the room.

The woman rose at once. Her eyes were very red, as if she had been crying. Half defiantly she asked if she might, for a moment, see the little girl, Pollyanna.

Miss Polly said no. She began to say it very sternly; but something in the woman's pleading eyes made her add the civil explanation that no one was allowed yet to see Pollyanna.

The woman hesitated; then a little brusquely she spoke. Her chin was still at a slightly defiant tilt.

"My name is Mrs. Payson—Mrs. Tom Payson. I presume you've heard of me—most of the good people in the town have—and maybe some of the

things you've heard ain't true. But never mind
that. It's about the little girl I came. I heard about
the accident, and — and it broke me all up. Last
week I heard how she couldn't ever walk again,
and — and I wished I could give up my two use-
lessly well legs for hers. She'd do more good
trotting around on 'em one hour than I could in
a hundred years. But never mind that. Legs ain't
always given to the one who can make the best use
of 'em, I notice."

She paused, and cleared her throat; but when she
resumed her voice was still husky.

" Maybe you don't know it, but I've seen a good
deal of that little girl of yours. We live on the Pendleton Hill road, and she used to go by often —
only she didn't always *go by*. She came in and
played with the kids and talked to me — and my
man, when he was home. She seemed to like it,
and to like us. She didn't know, I suspect, that
her kind of folks don't generally call on my kind.
Maybe if they *did* call more, Miss Harrington,
there wouldn't be so many — of my kind," she
added, with sudden bitterness.

" Be that as it may, she came; and she didn't
do herself no harm, and she did do us good — a
lot o' good. How much she won't know — nor

can't know, I hope; 'cause if she did, she'd know
other things — that I don't want her to know.

" But it's just this. It's been hard times with
us this year, in more ways than one. We've been
blue and discouraged — my man and me, and ready
for — 'most anything. We was reckoning on getting a divorce about now, and letting the kids —
well, we didn't know what we would do with the
kids. Then came the accident, and what we heard
about the little girl's never walking again. And
we got to thinking how she used to come and sit
on our doorstep and train with the kids, and laugh,
and — and just be glad. She was always being
glad about something; and then, one day, she told
us why, and about the game, you know; and tried
to coax us to play it.

" Well, we've heard now that she's fretting her
poor little life out of her, because she can't play
it no more — that there's nothing to be glad about.
And that's what I came to tell her to-day — that
maybe she can be a little glad for us, 'cause we've
decided to stick to each other, and play the game
ourselves. I knew she would be glad, because she
used to feel kind of bad — at things we said, sometimes. Just how the game is going to help us, I
can't say that I exactly see, yet; but maybe 'twill

Anyhow, we're going to try — 'cause she wanted us to. Will you tell her?"

"Yes, I will tell her," promised Miss Polly, a little faintly. Then, with sudden impulse, she stepped forward and held out her hand. "And thank you for coming, Mrs. Payson," she said simply.

The defiant chin fell. The lips above it trembled visibly. With an incoherently mumbled something, Mrs. Payson blindly clutched at the outstretched hand, turned, and fled.

The door had scarcely closed behind her before Miss Polly was confronting Nancy in the kitchen.

"Nancy!"

Miss Polly spoke sharply. The series of puzzling, disconcerting visits of the last few days, culminating as they had in the extraordinary experience of the afternoon, had strained her nerves to the snapping point. Not since Miss Pollyanna's accident had Nancy heard her mistress speak so sternly.

"Nancy, *will* you tell me what this absurd 'game' is that the whole town seems to be babbling about? And what, please, has my niece to do with it? *Why* does everybody, from Milly Snow to Mrs. Tom Payson, send word to her that they're 'playing it'? As near as I can judge, half the town are putting on blue ribbons, or stopping family quarrels, or learning to like something they never liked before, and all because of Pollyanna. I tried to ask the child herself about it, but I can't seem to make much headway, and of course I don't like to worry her — now. But from something I heard her say to you last night, I should judge you were one of them, too. Now *will* you tell me what it all means?"

To Miss Polly's surprise and dismay, Nancy burst into tears.

"It means that ever since last June that blessed child has jest been makin' the whole town glad, an' now they're turnin' 'round an' tryin' ter make her a little glad, too."

"Glad of what?"

"Just glad! That's the game."

Miss Polly actually stamped her foot.

"There you go like all the rest, Nancy. *What* game?"

Nancy lifted her chin. She faced her mistress and looked her squarely in the eye.

"I'll tell ye, ma'am. It's a game Miss Pollyanna's father learned her ter play. She got a pair of crutches once in a missionary barrel when she was wantin' a doll; an' she cried, of course, like

any child would. It seems 'twas then her father
told her that there wasn't ever anythin' but what
there was somethin' about it that you could be glad
about; an' that she could be glad about them
crutches."

"Glad for — *crutches!*" Miss Polly choked
back a sob — she was thinking of the helpless little
legs on the bed up-stairs.

"Yes'm. That's what I said, an' Miss Pollyanna
said that's what *she* said, too. But he told her she
could be glad — 'cause she *didn't need 'em.*"

"Oh-h!" cried Miss Polly.

"And after that she said he made a regular game
of it — findin' somethin' in everythin' ter be glad
about. An' she said ye could do it, too, and that
ye didn't seem ter mind not havin' the doll so much,
'cause ye was so glad ye *didn't* need the crutches.
An' they called it the 'jest bein' glad' game.
That's the game, ma'am. She's played it ever
since."

"But, how — how —" Miss Polly came to a
helpless pause.

"An' you'd be surprised ter find how cute it
works, ma'am, too," maintained Nancy, with almost the eagerness of Pollyanna herself. "I wish
I could tell ye what a lot she's done for mother an'

the folks out home. She's been ter see 'em, ye
know, twice, with me. She's made me glad, too,
on such a lot o' things — little things, an' big
things; an' it's made 'em so much easier. For
instance, I don't mind ' Nancy ' for a name half as
much since she told me I could be glad 'twa'n't
' Hephzibah.' An' there's Monday mornin's, too,
that I used ter hate so. She's actually made me glad
for Monday mornin's."

" Glad — for Monday mornings ! "

Nancy laughed.

" I know it does sound nutty, ma'am. But let
me tell ye. That blessed lamb found out I hated
Monday mornin's somethin' awful; an' what does
she up an' tell me one day but this : ' Well, anyhow,
Nancy, I should think you could be gladder on
Monday mornin' than on any other day in the
week, because 'twould be a whole *week* before
you'd have another one ! ' An' I'm blest if I hain't
thought of it ev'ry Monday mornin' since — an' it
has helped, ma'am. It made me laugh, anyhow,
ev'ry time I thought of it; an' laughin' helps, ye
know — it does, it does ! "

" But why hasn't — she told me — the game ? "
faltered Miss Polly. " Why has she made such a
mystery of it, when I asked her ? "

Nancy hesitated.

"Beggin' yer pardon, ma'am, you told her not ter speak of — her father; so she couldn't tell ye. 'Twas her father's game, ye see."

Miss Polly bit her lip.

"She wanted ter tell ye, first off," continued Nancy, a little unsteadily. "She wanted somebody ter play it with, ye know. That's why I begun it, — so she could have some one."

"And — and — these others?" Miss Polly's voice shook now.

"Oh, ev'rybody, 'most, knows it now, I guess. Anyhow, I should think they did from the way I'm hearin' of it ev'rywhere I go. Of course she told a lot, and they told the rest. Them things go, ye know, when they gets started. An' she was always so smilin' an' pleasant ter ev'ry one, an' so — so jest glad herself all the time, that they couldn't help knowin' it, anyhow. Now, since she's hurt, ev'rybody feels so bad — specially when they heard how bad *she* feels 'cause she can't find anythin' ter be glad about. An' so they've been comin' ev'ry day ter tell her how glad she's made *them*, hopin' that'll help some. Ye see, she's always wanted ev'rybody ter play the game with her."

"Well, I know somebody who'll play it — now,"

choked Miss Polly, as she turned and sped through the kitchen doorway.

Behind her, Nancy stood staring amazedly.

"Well, I'll believe anythin' — anythin' now," she muttered to herself. "Ye can't stump me with anythin' I wouldn't believe now — o' Miss Polly!"

A little later, in Pollyanna's roc n, the nurse left Miss Polly and Pollyanna alone together.

"And you've had still another caller to-day, my dear," announced Miss Polly, in a voice she vainly tried to steady. "Do you remember Mrs. Payson?"

"Mrs. Payson? Why, I reckon I do! She lives on the way to Mr. Pendleton's, and she's got the prettiest little girl baby three years old, and a boy 'most five. She's awfully nice, and so's her husband — only they don't seem to know how nice each other is. Sometimes they fight — I mean, they don't quite agree. They're poor, too, they say, and of course they don't ever have barrels, 'cause he isn't a missionary minister, you know, like — well, he isn't."

A faint color stole into Pollyanna's cheeks which was duplicated suddenly in those of her aunt.

"But she wears real pretty clothes, sometimes, in spite of their being so poor," resumed Pollyanna, in some haste. "And she's got perfectly beautiful rings with diamonds and rubies and emeralds in them; but she says she's got one ring too many, and that she's going to throw it away and get a divorce instead. What is a divorce, Aunt Polly? I'm afraid it isn't very nice, because she didn't look happy when she talked about it. And she said if she did get it, they wouldn't live there any more, and that Mr. Payson would go 'way off, and maybe the children, too. But I should think they'd rather keep the ring, even if they did have so many more. Shouldn't you? Aunt Polly, what is a divorce?"

"But they aren't going 'way off, dear," evaded Aunt Polly, hurriedly. "They're going to stay right there together."

"Oh, I'm so glad! Then they'll be there when I go up to see— O dear!" broke off the little girl, miserably. "Aunt Polly, why *can't* I remember that my legs don't go any more, and that I won't ever, ever go up to see Mr. Pendleton again?"

"There, there, don't," choked her aunt. "Perhaps you'll drive up sometime. But listen! I haven't told you, yet, all that Mrs. Payson said. She wanted me to tell you that they—they were going to stay together and to play the game, just as you wanted them to."

Pollyanna smiled through tear-wet eyes.

" Did they? Did they, really? Oh, I am glad of that! "

" Yes, she said she hoped you'd be. That's why she told you, to make you — *glad,* Pollyanna."

Pollyanna looked up quickly.

" Why, Aunt Polly, you — you spoke just as if you knew — *Do* you know about the game, Aunt Polly? "

" Yes, dear." Miss Polly sternly forced her voice to be cheerfully matter-of-fact. " Nancy told me. I think it's a beautiful game. I'm going to play it now — with you."

" Oh, Aunt Polly — *you?* I'm so glad! You see, I've really wanted you most of anybody, all the time."

Aunt Polly caught her breath a little sharply. It was even harder this time to keep her voice steady; but she did it.

" Yes, dear; and there are all those others, tco. Why, Pollyanna, I think all the town is playing that game now with you — even to the minister! I haven't had a chance to tell you, yet, but this morning I met Mr. Ford when I was down to the village, and he told me to say to you that just as soon as you could see him, he was coming to tell you that

he hadn't stopped being glad over those eight hundred rejoicing texts that you told him about. So
you see, dear, it's just you that have done it. The
whole town is playing the game, and the whole
town is wonderfully happier — and all because of
one little girl who taught the people a new game,
and how to play it."

Pollyanna clapped her hands.

" Oh, I'm so glad," she cried. Then, suddenly, a
wonderful light illumined her face. " Why, Aunt
Polly, there *is* something I can be glad about, after
all. I can be glad I've *had* my legs, anyway — else
I couldn't have done — that! "

CHAPTER XXIX

THROUGH AN OPEN WINDOW

ONE by one the short winter days came and went — but they were not short to Pollyanna. They were long, and sometimes full of pain. Very resolutely, these days, however, Pollyanna was turning a cheerful face toward whatever came. Was she not specially bound to play the game, now that Aunt Polly was playing it, too? And Aunt Polly found so many things to be glad about! It was Aunt Polly, too, who discovered the story one day about the two poor little waifs in a snow-storm who found a blown-down door to crawl under, and who wondered what poor folks did that didn't have any door! And it was Aunt Polly who brought home the other story that she had heard about the poor old lady who had only two teeth, but who was so glad that those two teeth " hit "!

Pollyanna now, like Mrs. Snow, was knitting wonderful things out of bright colored worsteds that trailed their cheery lengths across the white spread, and made Pollyanna — again like Mrs. Snow — so glad she had her hands and arms, anyway.

Pollyanna saw people now, occasionally, and always there were the loving messages from those she could not see; and always they brought her something new to think about — and Pollyanna needed new things to think about.

Once she had seen John Pendleton, and twice she had seen Jimmy Bean. John Pendleton had told her what a fine boy Jimmy was getting to be, and how well he was doing. Jimmy had told her what a first-rate home he had, and what bang-up " folks " Mr. Pendleton made; and both had said that it was all owing to her.

" Which makes me all the gladder, you know, that I *have* had my legs," Pollyanna confided to her aunt afterwards.

The winter passed, and spring came. The anxious watchers over Pollyanna's condition could see little change wrought by the prescribed treatment. There seemed every reason to believe, indeed, that Dr. Mead's worst fears would be realized — that Pollyanna would never walk again.

Beldingsville, of course, kept itself informed concerning Pollyanna; and of Beldingsville, one man in particular fumed and fretted himself into a fever of anxiety over the daily bulletins which he managed in some way to procure from the bed of suffering. As the days passed, however, and the news came to be no better, but rather worse, something besides anxiety began to show in the man's face: despair, and a very dogged determination, each fighting for the mastery. In the end, the dogged determination won; and it was then that Mr. John Pendleton, somewhat to his surprise, received one Saturday morning a call from Dr. Thomas Chilton.

" Pendleton," began the doctor, abruptly, " I've come to you because you, better than any one else in town, know something of my relations with Miss Polly Harrington."

John Pendleton was conscious that he must have started visibly — he did know something of the affair between Polly Harrington and Thomas Chilton, but the matter had not been mentioned between them for fifteen years, or more.

" Yes," he said, trying to make his voice sound concerned enough for sympathy, and not eager enough for curiosity. In a moment he saw that he need not have worried, however: the doctor was quite too intent on his errand to notice how that errand was received.

"Pendleton, I want to see that child. I want to make an examination. I *must* make an examination."

"Well — can't you?"

"*Can't* I! Pendleton, you know very well I haven't been inside that door for more than fifteen years. You don't know — but I will tell you — that the mistress of that house told me that the *next* time she *asked* me to enter it, I might take it that she was begging my pardon, and that all would be as before — which meant that she'd marry me. Perhaps you see her summoning me now — but I don't!"

"But couldn't you go — without a summons?"

The doctor frowned.

"Well, hardly. *I* have some pride, you know."

"But if you're so anxious — couldn't you swallow your pride and forget the quarrel —"

"Forget the quarrel!" interrupted the doctor, savagely. "I'm not talking of that kind of pride. So far as *that* is concerned, I'd go from here there

on my knees — or on my head — if that would do
any good. It's *professional* pride I'm talking
about. It's a case of sickness, and I'm a doctor. I can't butt in and say, ' Here, take me! ' —
can I? "

" Chilton, what *was* the quarrel? " demanded
Pendleton.

The doctor made an impatient gesture, and got to
his feet.

" What was it? What's any lovers' quarrel —
after it's over? " he snarled, pacing the room angrily. " A silly wrangle over the size of the moon
or the depth of a river, maybe — it might as well
be, so far as its having any real significance com-
pared to the years of misery that follow them!
Never mind the quarrel! So far as I am concerned,
I am willing to say there was no quarrel. Pendleton, I must see that child. It may mean life or
death. It will mean — I honestly believe — nine
chances out of ten that Pollyanna Whittier will
walk again! "

The words were spoken clearly, impressively;
and they were spoken just as the one who uttered
them had almost reached the open window near
John Pendleton's chair. Thus it happened that
very distinctly they reached the ears of a small boy

kneeling beneath the window on the ground outside.

Jimmy Bean, at his Saturday morning task of
pulling up the first little green weeds of the flower-
beds, sat up with ears and eyes wide open.

" Walk! Pollyanna!" John Pendleton was saying. "What do you mean?"

" I mean that from what I can hear and learn —
a mile from her bedside — that her case is very
much like one that a college friend of mine has just
helped. For years he's been making this sort of
thing a special study. I've kept in touch with him,
and studied, too, in a way. And from what I hear
— but I want to *see* the girl! "

John Pendleton came erect in his chair.

" You must see her, man! Couldn't you — say,
through Dr. Warren? "

The other shook his head.

" I'm afraid not. Warren has been very decent,
though. He told me himself that he suggested consultation with me at the first, but — Miss Harrington said no so decisively that he didn't dare venture
it again, even though he knew of my desire to see
the child. Lately, some of his best patients have
come over to me — so of course that ties my hands
still more effectually. But, Pendleton, I've got to

see that child! Think of what it may mean to her — if I do!"

"Yes, and think of what it will mean — if you don't!" retorted Pendleton.

"But how can I — without a direct request from her aunt? — which I'll never get!"

"She must be made to ask you!"

"How?"

"I don't know."

"No, I guess you don't — nor anybody else. She's too proud and too angry to ask me — after what she said years ago it would mean if she did ask me. But when I think of that child, doomed to lifelong misery, and when I think that maybe in my hands lies a chance of escape, but for that confounded nonsense we call pride and professional etiquette, I — " He did not finish his sentence, but with his hands thrust deep into his pockets, he turned and began to tramp up and down the room again, angrily.

"But if she could be made to see — to understand," urged John Pendleton.

"Yes; and who's going to do it?" demanded the doctor, with a savage turn.

"I don't know, I don't know," groaned the other, miserably.

Outside the window Jimmy Bean stirred suddenly. Up to now he had scarcely breathed, so intently had he listened to every word.

" Well, by Jinks, I know!" he whispered, exultingly. "*I'm* a-goin' ter do it!" And forthwith he rose to his feet, crept stealthily around the corner of the house, and ran with all his might down Pendleton Hill.

CHAPTER XXX

JIMMY TAKES THE HELM

"It's Jimmy Bean. He wants ter see ye, ma'am," announced Nancy in the doorway.

"Me?" rejoined Miss Polly, plainly surprised. "Are you sure he did not mean Miss Pollyanna? He may see her a few minutes to-day, if he likes."

"Yes'm. I told him. But he said it was you he wanted."

"Very well, I'll come down." And Miss Polly arose from her chair a little wearily.

In the sitting room she found waiting for her a round-eyed, flushed-faced boy, who began to speak at once.

"Ma'am, I s'pose it's dreadful — what I'm doin', an' what I'm sayin'; but I can't help it. It's for Pollyanna, and I'd walk over hot coals for her, or face you, or — or anythin' like that, any time. An' I think you would, too, if you thought there *was* a chance for her ter walk again. An' so that's why I come ter tell ye that as long as it's only pride an' et— et-somethin' that's keepin' Pollyanna from walkin', why I knew you *would* ask Dr. Chilton here if you understood — "

" Wh-at? " interrupted Miss Polly, the look of stupefaction on her face changing to one of angry indignation.

Jimmy sighed despairingly.

" There, I didn't mean ter make ye mad. That's why I begun by tellin' ye about her walkin' again. I thought you'd listen ter that."

" Jimmy, what are you talking about? "

Jimmy sighed again.

" That's what I'm tryin' ter tell ye."

" Well, then tell me. But begin at the beginning, and be sure I understand each thing as you go. Don't plunge into the middle of it as you did before — and mix everything all up! "

Jimmy wet his lips determinedly.

" Well, ter begin with, Dr. Chilton come ter see Mr. Pendleton, an' they talked in the library. Do you understand that? "

" Yes, Jimmy." Miss Polly's voice was rather faint.

" Well, the window was open, and I was weedin' the flower-bed under it; an' I heard 'em talk."

" Oh, Jimmy! *Listening?* "

" 'Twa'n't about me, an' 'twa'n't sneak listenin'," bridled Jimmy. " And I'm glad I listened. You will be when I tell ye. Why, it may make Polly-anna — walk ! "

" Jimmy, what do you mean? " Miss Polly was leaning forward eagerly.

" There, I told ye so," nodded Jimmy, con-tentedly. " Well, Dr. Chilton knows some doctor somewhere that can cure Pollyanna, he thinks — make her walk, ye know; but he can't tell sure till he *sees* her. And he wants ter see her somethin' awful, but he told Mr. Pendleton that you wouldn't let him."

Miss Polly's face turned very red.

" But, Jimmy, I — I can't — I couldn't! That is, I didn't know ! " Miss Polly was twisting her fin-gers together helplessly.

" Yes, an' that's what I come ter tell ye, so you *would* know," asserted Jimmy, eagerly. " They said that for some reason — I didn't rightly catch what — you wouldn't let Dr. Chilton come, an' you told Dr. Warren so; an' Dr. Chilton couldn't come himself, without you asked him, on account of pride an' professional et— et— well, et-somethin,' anyway. An' they was wishin' somebody could make you understand, only they didn't know who could; an' I was outside the winder, an' I says ter myself right away, ' By Jinks, I'll do it!' An' I come — an' have I made ye understand?"

" Yes; but, Jimmy, about that doctor," implored Miss Polly, feverishly. " Who was he? What did he do? Are they *sure* he could make Pollyanna walk?"

" I don't know who he was. They didn't say. Dr. Chilton knows him, an' he's just cured somebody just like her, Dr. Chilton thinks. Anyhow, they didn't seem ter be doin' no worryin' about *him*. 'Twas *you* they was worryin' about, 'cause you wouldn't let Dr. Chilton see her. An' say — you will let him come. won't you? — now you understand?"

Miss Polly turned her head from side to side. Her breath was coming in little uneven, rapid gasps. Jimmy, watching her with anxious eyes, thought she was going to cry. But she did not cry. After a minute she said brokenly:

" Yes — I'll let — Dr. Chilton — see her. Now run home, Jimmy — quick! I've got to speak to Dr. Warren. He's up-stairs now. I saw him drive in a few minutes ago."

A little later Dr. Warren was surprised to meet an agitated, flushed-faced Miss Polly in the hall.

He was still more surprised to hear the lady say, a little breathlessly:

"Dr. Warren, you asked me once to allow Dr. Chilton to be called in consultation, and — I refused. Since then I have reconsidered. I very much desire that you *should* call in Dr. Chilton. Will you not ask him at once — please? Thank you."

CHAPTER XXXI

A NEW UNCLE

THE next time Dr. Warren entered the chamber where Pollyanna lay watching the dancing shimmer of color on the ceiling, a tall, broad-shouldered man followed close behind him.

"Dr. Chilton! — oh, Dr. Chilton, how glad I am to see *you!*" cried Pollyanna. And at the joyous rapture of the voice, more than one pair of eyes in the room brimmed hot with sudden tears. "But, of course, if Aunt Polly doesn't want — "

"It is all right, my dear; don't worry," soothed Miss Polly, agitatedly, hurrying forward. "I have told Dr. Chilton that — that I want him to look you over — with Dr. Warren, this morning."

"Oh, then you asked him to come," murmured Pollyanna, contentedly.

"Yes, dear, I asked him. That is — " But it was too late. The adoring happiness that had leaped to Dr. Chilton's eyes was unmistakable, and Miss Polly had seen it. With very pink cheeks she turned and left the room hurriedly.

Over in the window the nurse and Dr. Warren were talking earnestly. Dr. Chilton held out both his hands to Pollyanna.

"Little girl, I'm thinking that one of the very gladdest jobs you ever did has been done to-day," he said in a voice shaken with emotion.

At twilight a wonderfully tremulous, wonderfully different Aunt Polly crept to Pollyanna's bedside. The nurse was at supper. They had the room to themselves.

"Pollyanna, dear, I'm going to tell you — the very first one of all. Some day I'm going to give Dr. Chilton to you for your — uncle. And it's you that have done it all. Oh, Pollyanna, I'm so — happy! And so — glad! — darling!"

Pollyanna began to clap her hands; but even as she brought her small palms together the first time, she stopped, and held them suspended.

"Aunt Polly, Aunt Polly, *were* you the woman's hand and heart he wanted so long ago? You were — I know you were! And that's what he meant by saying I'd done the gladdest job of all — to-day. I'm so glad! Why, Aunt Polly, I don't know but I'm so glad that I don't mind — even my legs, now!"

Aunt Polly swallowed a sob.

" Perhaps, some day, dear — " But Aunt Polly did not finish. Aunt Polly did not dare to tell, yet, the great hope that Dr. Chilton had put into her heart. But she did say this — and surely this was quite wonderful enough — to Pollyanna's mind:

" Pollyanna, next week you're going to take a journey. On a nice comfortable little bed you're going to be carried in cars and carriages to a great doctor who has a big house many miles from here made on purpose for just such people as you are. He's a dear friend of Dr. Chilton's, and we're going to see what he can do for you! "

CHAPTER XXXII

WHICH IS A LETTER FROM POLLYANNA

"DEAR AUNT POLLY AND UNCLE TOM: — Oh, I can — I can — I *can* walk! I did to-day all the way from my bed to the window! It was six steps. My, how good it was to be on legs again!

"All the doctors stood around and smiled, and all the nurses stood beside of them and cried. A lady in the next ward who walked last week first, peeked into the door, and another one who hopes she can walk next month, was invited in to the party, and she laid on my nurse's bed and clapped her hands. Even Black Tilly who washes the floor, looked through the piazza window and called me 'Honey, child' when she wasn't crying too much to call me anything.

"I don't see why they cried. *I* wanted to sing and shout and yell! Oh — oh — oh! Just think, I can walk — walk — *walk!* Now I don't mind being here almost ten months, and I didn't miss the wedding, anyhow. Wasn't that just like you, Aunt

Polly, to come on here and get married right beside my bed, so I could see you. You always do think of the gladdest things!

" Pretty soon, they say, I shall go home. I wish I could walk all the way there. I do. I don't think I shall ever want to ride anywhere any more. It will be so good just to walk. Oh, I'm so glad! I'm glad for everything. Why, I'm glad now I lost my legs for a while, for you never, never know how perfectly lovely legs are till you haven't got them — that go, I mean. I'm going to walk eight steps to-morrow.

" With heaps of love to everybody,

" POLLYANNA."

THE END.

CPSIA information can be obtained at www.ICGtesting.com
Printed in the USA
LVOW041651111111

254586LV00004B/15/P